D0184644

Kellie

KELLIE HARRINGTON
WITH RODDY DOYLE

SANDYCOVE

an imprint of

PENGUIN BOOKS

SANDYCOVE

UK | USA | Canada | Ireland | Australia
India | New Zealand | South Africa

Sandycove is part of the Penguin Random House group of companies
whose addresses can be found at global.penguinrandomhouse.com.

First published 2022
001

Copyright © Kellie Harrington and Roddy Doyle, 2022

The moral right of the authors has been asserted

Set in 13.5/16pt Garamond MT Std
Typeset by Jouve (UK), Milton Keynes
Printed and bound in Great Britain by Clays Ltd, Elcograf S.p.A.

The authorized representative in the EEA is Penguin Random House Ireland,
Morrison Chambers, 32 Nassau Street, Dublin D02 YH68

A CIP catalogue record for this book is available from the British Library

ISBN: 978–1–844–88607–4

To Mandy

I

We were running up the escalator with our bags full
of cameras and mascaras, holding hands and singing,
'They're not gonna get us!'

I was still in primary school, in sixth class, and I was drinking and experimenting – drinking anything that wasn't too expensive to buy. And taking pills. I was doing everything that wasn't what a normal child would do.

I was hanging around in the Clarence Street and Dunne Street flats. Sitting on the wall. There'd be me, Ango, Lizo, Lindsay, Linda, Jade. There'd be boys as well. David and Joe would have been there, and Paul – we called him Batman. We'd have a big radio, a three-in-one, and we'd put CDs in it and tapes, and we'd be listening to Hot FM, an illegal pirate station that played all the best tunes, the best house and dance music. The batteries were expensive enough, so we all had to chip in the money to get them in the Pound Shop on Talbot Street. Hot FM played all the great dance songs – Alice Deejay, Robert Miles's 'Children', '9PM', 'Sandstorm', 'The Logical Song', 'Scatman', 'Set You Free' by N-Trance; 'Summer Jam' – that was a big one. It was a great station. You could text in requests, and I'd be texting: Say hello to Lindsay, Lizo, Kellie and Ango, all sitting on the wall in the flats.

There were three blocks of flats, and a row of pram sheds at the front, and the wall. There was a big empty space in the middle, like a tarmac football pitch, and some of the lads from the flats would come in on stripped-down – stolen – bikes and they'd fly around, pulling wheelies and skids, and passing the bikes around to others to have a shot. The Garda would fly in and the lads would take a chase, and we'd be sitting there on the wall, watching it all happen in front of us.

We'd be sitting close in together, linking, because it was absolutely freezing; the steam was coming from our mouths. We'd be drinking the cans, with the radio on at full pelt. There'd be people from the flats giving out, even ringing the Garda to get them to come down and move us on. There was one way in from the bottom end of the flats, the Dunne Street end, and there were two ways in or out at the top. So there were three escape routes, if we needed to do a quick run. The Garda were going around in their cars or on their bikes, and if someone saw them, they'd go, 'Garda!' – giving everyone else the billy, the heads-up.

'Sketch!'

We'd grab the bags of cans and the radio, and run. Or we'd hide the cans and bottles, stay on the wall, lower the music when the Garda came, and we'd be, 'We haven't got the music loud – what're you talking about?'

They'd move us on – they'd try to. But we came back. They gave up. All we were doing was making noise and drinking. They had bigger things to be dealing with.

I was going through stuff that I didn't even know I was going through. My brain was wired differently, maybe. The first time I drank, or experimented, it made me feel good. I wanted to keep that feeling. I was escaping from myself, from the thoughts I was having. Dark thoughts – the feeling that I didn't belong. With the drinking and the drugs, those thoughts were gone. I just felt amazing. So I was doing it more, and more.

You're growing up and you see it – drug dealers all around

you. They were on every corner. The neighbours and parents were fighting to get them off the streets.

'What do we want?! Pushers out! When do we want it?! Now!'

The dealers didn't care who was watching them. They didn't care who they sold to. They didn't care how old you were.

My Ma and Da were telling me, 'Don't be doing this, don't be doing that.' They were telling me it was wrong and that I wasn't to be hanging around. But it wasn't like I was living in Blackrock or Dalkey. I was seeing it when I walked out our front door. I wasn't frightened of what was happening, but I knew it was wrong – and I knew that my Ma and Da were worried sick about me. I had three brothers and none of them gave my Ma an ounce of trouble. Just me.

This went on for a good while – years. I was drinking naggins of vodka, mixed with half a bottle of Coke in the Coke bottle, or Bulmers and Blue Wicked. I got the money for it all by shoplifting. Penneys mostly, but I'd get stuff out of other shops too. And I did a bit of babysitting. I looked after two of my cousins for a few hours on a Friday or Saturday. I'd be saving the money and using it on the weekends.

Me and my friend Donna went into Penneys and Topshop and Miss Selfridge dressed the exact same, like twins, in clothes we'd robbed from other shops, and we were walking around the shop, not a care in the world, and dropping clothes into our bags. That was how brazen we were. It was like, 'I don't care.' I was taking tops, jumpers, shoes, bobbins, hairbands – anything that was there and that I liked. We'd put the clothes on and walk out of the shop with four pairs of trousers and six tops underneath the clothes we'd worn in. We sold most of the stolen clothes that we were wearing. We always found someone to buy them.

Ango – Angelina – was my best friend growing up. We were thick as thieves – literally. We were in Tesco's once, taking disposable cameras and hair dye and hairspray. We were running up the escalator with our bags full of cameras and mascaras, holding hands and singing, 'They're not gonna get us!' – the t.A.T.u. song from back then.

I'd be walking out of the shop wondering, 'Fuck – are they going to catch me now?' It was the adrenaline rush – the same rush I get when I step into the ring. I loved it.

Throughout it all, my Ma would have been thinking, 'She's mixing with the wrong crowd,' and she'd have been blaming it on them. But I never saw it that way. I was the one who wanted to do stuff like that – to drink, to take the drugs, to shoplift. No one had me by the hand, saying, 'This is what you're going to do today, Kellie.'

My head was just so messed up. When kids are developing they're all over the shop. They don't know whether they're coming or going. I didn't know who I was. I was streetwise; or I thought I was. But I was immature. I definitely wasn't a normal thirteen- or fourteen-year-old. I thought everyone was out to get me and that it was everyone else's fault. Getting into trouble in school – it was never my fault. But I was always quiet – at least, I think I was. I didn't stand out. The whole crowd stood out. There were gangs of us. There was no real head honcho – we were all doing the same thing. Stuff that was wrong but felt good. Everything was chaotic.

I was caught shoplifting in Penneys on Mary Street twice, and I was arrested both times. The first time I was with Donna. The only reason we were caught was because my bag ripped in the shop and I had the neck to go up to the counter and ask the lady at the till for a new one. We were brought to Store Street Garda Station. My Ma dragged me home. She was shouting at me – I can't remember what she was saying. I was grounded but they couldn't keep me in for long; I just did their heads in. They had to let me back out. They'd lock the door sometimes, but I'd manage to escape. I'd take off, like a bat out of hell. I was out of control.

I'd be fighting with my brothers, mostly with my big brother, Christopher. We battered each other. And it was great – it was brilliant. We'd batter the shit out of each other.

My Da would leave us to it.

'If you want to act like that, off you go.'

And I'd mess-fight with my Da in the kitchen.

My Ma would always warn me, 'Now, Kellie – you're going to end up crying. It'll get too serious.'

'No, no, it won't. Come on, Da, come on, Da.'

My Da's a southpaw, so I always say that I learnt everything I know about boxing from sparring with him. I was fast and flighty on my feet and I'd be clattering him, getting in, and out. In a little kitchen, with the chip pan on full whack! He'd be hitting me back – solid. I'd end up crying.

My Ma would be there, 'I told you! He doesn't know how to play. I told you not to be messing!'

I'd smack him the next day and we'd be off again.

'No,' he'd say. 'You can't handle it – you're always whingeing.'

'I won't, I won't, Da – I swear I won't.'

But I really wasn't getting on with my brothers. They were into football, and I wasn't. I knew that Olivia O'Toole, who'd played football for Ireland, only lived down the road. But I associated football with my brothers and it just wasn't me; it wasn't what I wanted. I didn't feel like I fitted in. I hated it – football was on in the house 24/7, and my Da would be bringing the boys off to their matches. I'd none of that. Even if there had been women's football, I wouldn't have done it – because it was what they did.

But none of them boxed.

*

There are boxing clubs on every corner of the inner city. There are no hockey clubs, there are no tennis clubs. But I'd see boys going to boxing, with their bags across their shoulders. And throughout all of this – me going on a mad one – I looked at them and I always knew they were doing something good with their lives. They were all boys, no girls.

One of the coaches from the local club, Corinthians Boxing Club, lived where I was hanging around. His name was Joey O'Brien, and his flat faced the wall that me and my friends would be sitting on. I found out he was a coach and, straight away, I began to talk to him about boxing and fitness. I knocked up to his house and I asked him, 'Any chance of me joining the boxing club?'

He said no: the secretary of the club wouldn't allow girls to come down and join.

My Da's friend Martin Lawless lived in Whitehall, and he had a shed in the back of the house with boxing bags in it, and weights. Martin wasn't involved in a boxing club, which I always say was a waste of a good coach. Just a few sessions with Martin on the bags and on the pads showed me the basics. I loved it and I wanted more, so I kept knocking on Joey's door.

'What's the story, Joey? Will I be allowed join?'

'I asked the secretary, Kellie, but he's saying no.'

During this time, I was in and out of Swan Youth Service – the youth club in St Agatha's Hall, across from my old primary school. I told Eibhlin Harrington – no relation – there, 'I want to start boxing and I can't get into Corinthians.'

Eibhlin got in contact with Dublin Docklands Boxing Club – they're based in Seville Place, very near my house – and she asked for a coach to come and meet us. So this man came up and he was taken aback to see that it was a group of girls who wanted to box. Especially me; I really, really wanted to box.

I think that coach is in a boxing club in Meath now and he has a daughter who boxes for him but, back then, he was like, 'Oh, we don't take girls.' When I won my medal in the World Championships in 2018, the same fella turned up at the airport for the homecoming, with his daughter. Me being me, I saw him and I was like, 'Jesus Christ – do you remember when you wouldn't let me into your boxing club? You said you wouldn't take girls. And here you are now – with your daughter.'

An elephant never forgets.

The second time I was caught shoplifting in Penneys I was brought to Store Street Garda Station again. It was my Da who came up and collected me the second time. My Da is very quiet; he doesn't say a whole lot. My Ma would be more of the panicker, causing ructions.

'She can't be doing this – Christy, you have to do something.'

But he never did. Like, what could he do? But then, he *did* do something. He got on the phone to his sister in England.

By that time I was in secondary school, in Larkin Community College, off Seán McDermott Street. It's a blur to me, the way things happened – but I got sent over to London. To my auntie. My parents didn't know what to do with me, so sending me there was an act of desperation: 'Just get her out of the country.'

I'd stayed with my other auntie, Paula, and my Uncle Derek, up in Richmond Cottages, for a while. They had two girls, Jennifer and Shaunagh, and a boy, Derek. I wasn't *living* living there; it was for periods of time – now and again.

I just never got on with my Ma when I was going through

all of this stuff. I used to imagine – like a lot of kids – that the world was out to get me and the teachers were out to get me; everyone was out to get me. And I thought my Ma was the same. I was like, 'You love your blue-eyed boys!' Kids clash with their parents and my Ma was the one I clashed with. Maybe it's because we're so alike – I don't know.

I knew why my parents were sending me over to England. I didn't feel rejected or that I was being sent into exile. My head was very messed up – I was all over the place. I knew they were trying to take me away from everything I was doing.

I told my cousin, Shaunagh, that I was going to London, and we were both crying. She told me that everything would be all right and that I'd be back soon enough. Shaunagh gave me her bed when I stayed in Richmond Cottages, even though she was only a year older than me, and she slept on the floor. She'd be getting her bed back when I left!

Paula flew over with me to London, and dropped me off in Whetstone, north London, with my other auntie, Geraldine. I was there for four months, living with four other girls, my cousins, and Geraldine – she's my Da's sister – and her husband, David. It was great, because my cousins – Janine, Jade, Mia and Mei – were normal kids doing normal kids' stuff. They were around the same age as me. I had my own room, although it wasn't a proper bedroom. It was kind of a garage, and they'd put a curtain up for me. So I had my own little space behind the curtain, and I put posters up – Tupac, Biggie, Bob Marley. There was talk of me starting school over there.

I knew nobody, except my cousins. I wasn't going to be drinking or getting into trouble. Geraldine was so strict, I'd have been afraid to cross her. She'd have leathered the arse off me if I'd done anything wrong. With my parents, I had no fear. With Geraldine, though, I was on my best behaviour. As for shoplifting, I'd have been terrified of getting caught over there. I was in a different country. What if I ended up in a children's prison? That was how I was thinking. *And* I knew why I was there: to stop doing what I'd been doing. It wasn't punishment; they were trying to save me.

I got on well with my cousins. But I started to miss home and to miss my Ma and Da. I'd ring them every day, and I wrote letters to Shaunagh: *How are you doing and what's happening in Ireland? I miss yis. I can't wait to see yis.* They had cats and I was asking how the cats were. I'd put stickers on the letters, little pictures of animals. Real innocent kid's stuff.

I wasn't going to school, so during the day I'd walk up the high street, or do the shopping on the High Road with my Auntie Geraldine. Her husband, David – my uncle – is Chinese, and they had a restaurant in Chinatown, in the middle of London. He'd bring us in, me and my cousins, and we'd have dinner there. I used to love it, because it was so different. I'd feel like the bee's knees – sophisticated. I'd be like, 'Can I get some green tea, please?' I didn't like it but I just wanted to be part of all this and to do what everyone else was doing.

They'd go to see their Chinese nanny. She didn't speak a word of English, but I was convinced that she could understand it. I liked her – probably because she didn't speak to me. She was very friendly. I always got that sense of kindliness off David's side of the family, the Lams. They rallied around the kids; there was a big fuss made about them, and about me, whenever we went anywhere.

I remember once, we went into Chinatown and the whole family was there. Everyone else seemed to be ordering the chicken soup, so I ordered it as well. The soup came out, and it was watery – you could see right through it – and there were two chicken's feet at the bottom of the bowl. I nearly

9

died when I saw them. I didn't say anything; I was afraid to. It was their culture; I didn't want to be whingeing. But I was whispering to my cousins, because they weren't eating it either.

So I was like, 'The chicken soup – what am I going to do?'

'Just move it to the side, like.'

We just kept moving the bowls around, away from us. The adults at the table knew exactly what we were doing and I'd say they were laughing at us.

They had a cousin or uncle, Andrew, who did martial arts. I remember asking him lots of questions. I was quite inspired by him.

I'd meet my cousins after school, and we'd do each other's make-up. It was just cheap make-up that the girls had. We'd put eyeshadow on me; we'd think we were make-up artists, practising. We'd be doing each other's hair, plaiting and crimping, putting nail varnish on our fingernails and toes. I was with girls, not my brothers, and I loved it. I was a child again.

2

She never hit me, that girl – but she frightened the
life out of me by saying she was going to kill me.
She had a real fighting mouth on her.

My little brother, Joel, was born on my birthday, 11 December, seven years after me. I already had two brothers and I'd been going around for weeks, boasting, 'Yes! I'm having a baby sister, I'm having a baby sister!'

My Auntie Rosaleen got a phone call off my Da during the night, to tell her that my Ma had gone into labour. Rosaleen shouted up the stairs to my cousin Tanya, telling her to get up. Tanya got up and put on her school uniform, because she thought she was being called for school. She came down the stairs.

'Yvonne's having the baby – it's not school time.'

Tanya had to go to our house with Rosaleen, because Rosaleen couldn't leave her there while she was minding me and the lads, while Ma and Da were up in the Rotunda.

Rosaleen woke us up and told us the news that Ma was after having the baby. I was jumping up and down on the bed.

'I'm getting a sister for a birthday present!'

But the boys knew – my Auntie had told them. They were whispering to each other.

'Like – how're we going to tell her? It's not a bleedin' sister, it's another brother.'

It was Tanya who broke the news to me.

'Ah, no—!'

I was bawling my eyes out. I love Joel to bits now, but at the time I wasn't happy.

'I'll be your big sister if you want,' said Tanya.

'Eh – okay.'

We went in to the Rotunda to see him. He was crying, howling – a little whinger, he was. But he was my birthday present, a baby brother instead of a baby sister. And I told everybody.

'I got a new brother for me birthday present.'

I was born in the Rotunda myself, on 11th December 1989. At first, we lived in Richmond Cottages, where my parents were renting the top half of a house. There was myself and my older brother, Christopher. My Auntie Paula and my Uncle Derek – he's my Ma's brother – lived right across the road, with the two children they had then, Shaunagh and Jennifer. I've no memories of living there.

I was less than a year old when my Ma and Da were offered a house from Dublin City Council and we moved to Portland Row. That's where I grew up.

Kellie Anne is my full name – Kellie Anne Harrington. My Da's side of the family all call me Kellie Anne. I'd ring my Nanny Harrington all the time, and she'd always be, 'Ah, hellooo, Kellie Anne!'

Some of the girls in primary school called me Kellie Anne as well. The teacher would be calling out the roll.

'Kellie Anne Harrington?'

'*Anseo.*' Here.

Or:

'Kellie Anne Harrington? Kellie Anne Harrington?'

'She's hiding around in the flats, teacher.'

Everyone else just calls me Kellie. But when I'm boxing,

it's always Kellie Anne Harrington, because they go off your passport and the name – Kellie Anne Harrington – comes up on a big screen for all major competitions.

My Da is Christopher – Christy. My Ma is Yvonne. She was a Duffy. She grew up in Hardwicke Street, behind Dorset Street, in a two-bedroom flat. There were nine of them in the family, the seven children in one bedroom and their Ma and Da in the other. My Ma and her friend Susan Murphy were mad into dogs, and they kept them in the Hardwicke Street flats pram shed. At one stage, they had a German shepherd and it had nine pups. They were well looked after in the pram shed. I didn't lick my love for dogs off a rock.

There were twelve children on my Da's side. His family originally came from Celbridge, in Kildare, and they upped sticks and moved to Finglas. So my Da grew up in Finglas and my Ma grew up in town.

My Da would bring us out to visit my Nanny and Grandda. I loved going out to Finglas. It felt like we were going out to the countryside. We'd get on the number 40 bus, on Parnell Street. It would leave us at the top of Mellowes Road and we'd walk down to Mellowes Avenue. My Nanny lived in number 118. I loved going out there to see her.

My Grandda would be there too.

'How's it going, Mary Jane? How're you doing today?'

He called every one of us names that weren't our actual names. I remember thinking, 'He doesn't even know my name.'

One day, I asked my Nanny Harrington about it.

'Nanny – does my Grandda know my name is Kellie Anne, like?'

'Of course he knows your name is Kellie Anne – that's just your Grandda.'

Once after that, he called me Kellie Anne, and I nearly died. 'Oh my God, he actually said my name.' But then he started calling me different names again.

There are some things that we never forget, and me and my brothers will never forget the smell of cabbage in my Nanny's house. We'd be nearly sick but, as we got older, I'd be looking forward to my Nanny putting the dinner on, a bit of bacon and cabbage with mashed potatoes.

There used to be a fruit and veg man called Martin who'd come around in his van, and my Nanny would get a box of fruit and veg for us. My Da would take it home on the bus, or my Grandda would bring it for us in his car. He used to drink in Bermingham's pub, on Dorset Street, and sometimes he'd drop us back into town. He drove this kind of big version of a Mini and he wore a hat like a bus driver's cap – although he wasn't a bus driver. In the car with the three boys, I'd be scarlet for my life in case any of my friends saw me in this thing. I would have been mortified. As soon as he stopped it, I'd be out in a flash and into the house.

I've loads of cousins, because the family was so big, and everyone used to go to my Nanny's on Sundays. There'd be John and Sarah, Hazel, Jenny, Raymond, Luke, Caroline, Jade, and Muxima and Nzinga. We'd play out on the road – chasing and stuck-in-the-mud.

My Nanny had loads of wild cats at the back of the house and she always fed them. There was a sliding door from the kitchen to the garden, and the cats would come up to the door and rub their little bodies against it, like they were asking, 'Is there any food going?' When we opened the door, they'd back off a bit and just look up at us, waiting. I'd get them to come up and take the food from my hand, and my Nanny did it too; they ate everything. She always said that once you had cats you'd never have rats. But I kind of stopped believing that because the cats were so well fed; they were stuffed.

The Duffys – that's the side of the family that no one ever talks about! I wasn't as close to my Nanny Duffy as I was to my Nanny Harrington. My Grandda Duffy died before I was born.

My Ma was close to her sister, Rosaleen. Rosaleen's kids, Hubert, who I called 'Huba', and Tanya, were like my brother and sister when I was growing up. When I was seven or eight, Huba and his friend took me to see the Spice Girls' movie, *Spice World*; I loved the Spice Girls. But I think they took me because they wanted to see it themselves, and I was their excuse.

I had another little cousin called Kirsty, and she used to stay either in Rosaleen's or my Ma's house most weekends. My Ma would crimp our hair; she'd have an old bed sheet and she'd tear it into strips and put them in our hair. Every time Kirsty came to the house something unlucky would happen. One time, a wardrobe came down on top of her. She was all right, but it could have killed her. Another time, we were on the North Strand, and she got the smack of a bike. The handlebars whacked right into her forehead. She was panned out on the ground.

I loved primary school – absolutely loved it. I went to St Vincent's Girls' National School on William Street, right across from St Agatha's Church. I loved being with my friends there; the craic in the classroom was always great. Me and my classmates, Robyn, Gero and Kellie Anne, who had the same name as me – we'd have some buzz. We gave the teachers a bit of stick, but it was always healthy. There was Miss Ruane, Miss Reid, Miss O'Connor – she's the principal now. They were brilliant. There was Miss Hynes. I met her, just before

15

the Olympics, in a shop in Blackrock. She came up and congratulated me.

'You've come a long way.'

It was lovely to hear that, from a teacher. I was surprised she even remembered me.

There was a breakfast club, and that made me want to go to school even more; it was absolutely deadly. I'd go in early, and up to the top of the stairs, and I'd get my bowl of Cornflakes or Rice Krispies or Coco Pops, and there was juice on the table. And I'd be waiting on the toast – everyone *loved* the toast, with the butter on it. It was the same toast that we got at home but it tasted so much better. We'd be in the breakfast room till the very last minute. It was like closing time in the pub; there'd be a dash for the juice. Mary who did the breakfasts would be trying to get us out, to go to our classes.

'Hold on, hold on – I'm just finishing me juice!'

We nearly had to be dragged out.

When we got to sixth class – the last year – we got to mind the junior infants and senior infants on the big lunchbreak. There were two girls designated to mind each class. We'd get them into their line and bring them out to the yard, and back in, and the teacher would take over again. We'd take turns going around the classes with the milk and bread baskets. I always tried to get selected to do it on Friday, because we got chocolate muffins on a Friday. I'd bring stuff home, the milk from school, the muffins, and, if there were any left, sandwiches. I don't know if anyone ever ate the sandwiches.

The church, St Agatha's, faced the school, and St Agatha's Youth Club was right next to the church. So there was the youth club, there was the school and there was the church, all together. I was in the church choir and my friends Jessica and Jade – who were twins – were in it too. Jade had the voice of an angel; she was amazing. She still sings, in the Dublin

Gospel Choir. I went to choir practice maybe twice a week, and I'd sing on a Sunday, at mass. I was always told to come straight home for my dinner after mass. My Ma and Da never went to mass to hear the choir, so we can't have been *that* good.

St Agatha's Youth Club had a dance class. I went in to do the dancing, but I was so nervous that I wet myself.

That was it; I never went back. I wonder now why I wasn't like that with boxing. Today, I'm first up on the dance floor. But disco dancing, formal moves – I couldn't do it.

I remember making my First Holy Communion. That was a big pay day. I remember going over to Thomas Street with my Ma, to a shop that sold the dresses, Jas Fagan's, and we picked out the dress and the veil. Now, when I think of it, it's 'Oh my God': they're horrendous things, mini wedding dresses. I think it cost about £500, which was massive money for a dress that was never going to be across my back again. But I couldn't wait to get it on.

The day itself – it was going around to everyone's houses, collecting the winnings. As soon as I got out of a house, I'd open the card to see what was in it, and I'd put the money into the little communion bag that came with my dress and I'd hand over the card to my Ma or Da. With the amount of aunts and uncles I had, I was really in the money. I've no idea what I spent it on, or if I was let keep all of it. I bought the dinner for everybody that night, from Luigi's chipper on the North Strand. I counted my money, over and over – and over.

One Christmas I got a Barbie house. It must have been four foot high. There was nothing in it; it was just a big plastic house. I loved it. There was a little door, and I could fit through it and curl up into a ball. Eventually, I was allowed to take it outside, and myself and my friends, Jessica and Jade, Linda Mangan, who lived around on Dunne Street, and Sarah Dunne, who lived further up Portland Row – we dragged the house around the corner to the tarmac football pitch that was behind my house. We had our Barbies with us and we played for hours. Some of the men from the Lido, the Chinese takeaway, and from Luigi's chipper would come out; the back doors of their places led straight onto the pitch, and they'd be playing basketball or football while we'd be playing with our Barbies and chatting away to them. Sometimes we'd buy sweets and stuff in Davida's shop, on the North Strand, and we'd pretend that the Barbie house was a little shop, and we'd sell the stuff that we'd bought. The lads playing the football would buy the sweets; they'd pretend they were our customers.

Around the corner, just off the North Strand, there used to be old folks' homes. We called the building the Grannyer. There was no one living there any more, so the building was an 'eegah' – our name for a broken-down house. Myself and Linda Mangan used to climb into it and play. We were doing nothing, really, but it was the excitement: we knew we weren't meant to be in there.

Me and Linda knocked at my door, and my Da answered.

'Da – we're going around to the Grannyer.'

'Grand.'

'We're going round to the eegah in the Grannyer.'

'Grand – bring me back a Granny Smith apple.'

Me and Linda were like, 'Oh – he's letting us go round to the eegah!'

He had no clue what an eegah was.

I was with my mates Jessica and Jade, one day.

'We'll bring the dogs for a walk.'

The twins had a West Highland terrier, a male, and we had a scraggly little terrier, Cindy. She was absolutely gorgeous; she looked like a fox. So I went home and got her. And off we go, up to Our Lady's Park in Drumcondra. My Da used to bring us there, when I was small. There are steps down to the river – the Tolka – and there we were, paddling, in and out of the water.

I said, 'I'd love to have pups. Let's see if they can have pups.'

Dogs have to come into heat to breed. But I hadn't a clue, so it must have been pure coincidence: Cindy was in heat. The dogs started to mate and they got stuck. We had no idea, really, of what we were looking at.

'They're stuck! What do we do, like?!'

Someone shouted, 'You have to throw water over them!'

We were trying to scoop water out of the Tolka and throw it onto the dogs. They separated, eventually. And we went home. I never said anything to my Ma about what we'd done.

Weeks later, I'd totally forgotten about it. Me and all my mates were standing outside Davida's. It was an old-fashioned shop where you could just go in and say, 'Can I've twenty Benson and Hedges, please, and my Ma will fix you up on Friday.' It was where we went for our sweets. We were hanging around there, and outside the chipper.

My Ma came around the corner, to get her messages, and she saw me.

'Kellie—!'

I went over to her.

'See, you,' she goes. 'You never told me! There's fuckin' pups flyin' around the back garden!'

I was screaming; I was delighted. I ran around to the house. Cindy had had four or five lovely, fluffy little pups. They were gorgeous. But I never got to keep one of them.

*

St Agatha's Church was around the corner, and if we heard that there was a wedding on, we made sure we were there for the grushie.

'A wedding! Grushie!'

We rarely knew the people who were getting married but we'd be standing outside the church, going, 'Is there a grushie? Is there a grushie? Here, mister – are you doing a grushie?'

The bride and groom would come out of the church and they'd have their hands – both hands – full of coins, and they'd fling them into the air. It wasn't just little kids like us who were waiting. There'd be people much bigger than us, hundreds of them, all trying to get at the money, feet stamping all around us. Our fingers would be black and blue by the time all the coins had been grabbed.

Then we'd go straight into Davida's, around the corner from the church. I'd get my Capri-Sun, my packet of crisps, my Chomp, my fizzy cola lolly.

'Can I get the rest in jellies, please?'

Then it was back out the door, delighted with your life.

On Sundays, on Croke Park days, when there was a match, Portland Row was a little goldmine for parking cars. It's mad really – who'd let an eight-year-old mind their car? But it does make some kind of sense. If anybody was messing with the car, the eight-year-old would run into the house and go, 'Ma, Ma – there's someone touching my car!'

We'd be doing the parking, myself and Christopher Flood and J.J. Mangan, and my brother, Christopher. They – the boys – hated me being involved. But I didn't care.

'This is *my* car parking space!'

'No, *we're* parking the cars, *we're* minding them.'

There'd be killings on Portland Row over who owned what space. I'd be happy enough if I got one car. I'd be out with my newspaper rolled up, trying to get the passing car to take my space. But there'd be someone up the other end of the road, going, 'No, no – park up here! I've a garden here!'

I didn't have a garden but I'd ask Mrs Deery.

'Can I park in your garden today?'

She'd be looking at me.

'Park what, like?'

'A car, like – is it all right if I park someone's car in your garden?'

'No problem, Kellie.'

'Can I park one outside at the pole as well?'

'No problem, Kellie.'

I'd get four or five pounds for each car, and that was loads. Sometimes the owner would give me half the money and say, 'I'll give you the rest when I come back.'

If they gave me the full amount, I'd be gone. I'd buy a load of sweets and I'd be sitting inside, watching something on the telly.

'Da – will you look outside and see if that grey car is all right?'

But nothing ever happened any of the cars. There was a bus once, and the driver parked it; he took up a load of our spaces and he didn't come across with the spondulies – the money. We had nothing to do with it but, while he was on the bus, asleep, the bus was broken into.

'Aha – you should've let us mind your bus.'

Parking the cars – it's a real tradition. Some of the boys who did it when I did still park the cars on Croke Park days.

My Da used to work in Premier Dairies, and he'd bring home boxes of cereals – the miniature ones – and cartons of orange juice and cranberry juice. He'd give them to me.

'Here you go.'

And I'd take them and I'd go around the doors and sell

them. They'd be gone in a second; people would bite the hand off me for them.

Myself and Jessica and Jade made a sponsor card, for a skipathon that I was supposed to be doing for the school, a fundraiser. We forged it; there was no skipathon. But we went around the doors.

'Will you sponsor me?'

Some of the neighbours sponsored me, just to entertain me – to fool me. There was a woman Carmel, she lived in number 24. I knocked on her door.

'Carmel, will you sponsor me – for me skipathon in school?'

She sponsored me a pound or two. I was delighted. But she knocked up to my Ma and Da and she ratted me out.

'Jesus, Kellie – what are you doing?'

Carmel reminded me of that, later, when I'd come back from the World Championships or some other tournament, with my medal.

'I remember you when you were a little fucker, with your made-up sponsor cards an' all.'

Half the neighbours knew – maybe all of them did – that the sponsor cards weren't real. But they probably thought, 'Jesus, God loves a trier. Here you go – here's fifty pence for you.'

I've been wheeling and dealing all my life.

Christopher had a PlayStation – he's four years older than me. I only played two things, Crash Bandicoot and Rayman, but I'd only be able to play them if he wasn't there. He wouldn't let me on the PlayStation because I'd be taking the CDs out and putting them into the wrong boxes, and all that craic.

I loved Nickelodeon. I'd watch *Kenan & Kel, Sister, Sister,*

Sabrina the Teenage Witch, *Saved by the Bell*. And I loved *CatDog* – 'Just a feline canine little CatDog!' I used to love *Rugrats*, and *Hey Arnold!* – 'Hey Arnold – football head!' I'd come in from school and my Ma would have a bag of sweets. We'd sit down, eat the sweets and watch our programmes. My teeth are full of fillings because of my Ma – but I never complained.

There were only two bedrooms in our house, one for my parents and one for my brothers and me. We had a set of bunk beds on each side of the room. Christopher was on the top bunk, above me. I'd kick my feet up – the wooden slats under his mattress were loose. I'd lie flat on my bed and lift my feet, and I'd be kicking and pushing the slats, pestering the life out of him.

'Stop it! Ma – tell her!'

There'd be murder in the house. I'd be nearly wetting myself, laughing, because he'd be raging. I got great craic out of it.

I had this doll. It was huge, the same size as myself, maybe even bigger. It was a scary-looking thing; I didn't even have a name for it. But Christopher was terrified of it, and I loved the fact that he was terrified. I think he was seeing Chucky from *Child's Play* when he looked at that doll. I'd bring it into the bedroom when we were going to bed and I'd stand it in the corner. Christopher would be calling to my Ma.

'Ma – get that thing out of the room!'

She'd bring it out and leave it on the landing. I'd settle down for a while, then I'd go out and I'd bring it back in. In the end, we had to get rid of it.

As we got older, it wasn't ideal having the three boys – Christopher, Aaron and Joel – and a girl in the one room. They were going through puberty; I was going through puberty. I was constantly saying, 'I want to get the attic converted, I want to move out of this room, I want to move out of this house – I don't want to be in this room with them any more.'

So my Da partitioned the room, and made a smaller room for me. It was a shoebox – even smaller than a shoebox. But it was mine.

I said, 'Da, will you put my bed up on the wall?'

'How will we do that?'

We worked it out. The room was the same width as the mattress, so he hammered a wooden frame around the three walls, and the slats and the mattress went on top of it.

I had my little ladder from my old bunk bed, up to the mattress. And underneath, I had a blow-up chair. I thought it was the business. I felt sophisticated, like it was my office. It was class.

A girl from Sheriff Street used to come up every now and again to me and my mates, Jessica and Jade – in 23 Portland Row. We'd be playing in the garden.

This girl and her friends would stop at the gate.

'What did you say about my Ma?'

I didn't know what she was on about.

'I didn't say anything about your Ma.'

'You fuckin' did – she told me an' all.'

She'd be pointing at her mate. But her mate was standing there, clueless. She was just being a bully, that girl, inventing an excuse to bully me. And I'd be terrified. I was ten or eleven when it happened. I must have looked like a little victim then. I'd always try to talk my way out of a fight, but if you put your hand on me you were sorry. She never hit me, that girl – but she frightened the life out of me by saying she was going to kill me. She had a real fighting mouth on her.

I think it's one of the reasons I wanted to get into the boxing. I wasn't afraid of a fight, but I was terrified of her.

Me and the twins got caught shoplifting in Eason's. Robbing fridge magnets. They let us go but told us that they were going to tell our parents.

'They're going to tell our Ma and Da what we done,' I said. 'That's it – we'll have to run away. I'll get the food.'

I went home and got the Wagon Wheels and the Kool Kidz drinks and we were all set to go to St Anne's Park and live in the trees.

3

So I'm in the ring, my first fight ever. My nerves are
absolutely gone. I hit the girl, Caroline O'Reilly,
and I go, 'Oh – sorry, sorry!'

My Ma got a dog while I was away, and I named the dog
before I even met her. I called her Chas, after Chas Dingle,
because I was watching *Emmerdale* with my cousins in London. I'd been away for four months. I was homesick, and I
was dying to see the new dog.

I was phoning home every day.

'Can I come home?'

'Only if you're not going to start messing again.'

I said I wouldn't. I made a lot of promises.

I don't remember coming back from London. But I do
remember the dog. Chas was a bull mastiff – they're huge,
slobbery dogs. And she was brilliant. I wasn't allowed to take
her out for a walk but, eventually, my Da gave in.

My Ma was warning him.

'Make sure that choke is on proper, Christy.'

He helped me to put the choke lead on her – and we were
out the door, me and Chas, gone.

I was tall but thin, a little splint, and Chas was massive;
she must have been about forty kilos. She could have pulled
me to Timbuktu if she'd wanted to. She got a chicken breast
portion into her mouth, near the chipper. Someone's bag
must have been soaked with vinegar and it burst and the

chicken fell through, onto the path. I was trying to hold Chas between my legs so I could get the chicken portion out of her mouth. She backed out from my grip – she reversed – and came out of the choke collar. It must have been too loose.

She ran up Portland Row. I was screaming, chasing her – and she got the smack of a car. She got back up and ran, with the chicken breast still in her mouth. I eventually got her into a garden and was able to get the choke back on her. The chicken was gone; she'd necked it.

My Ma and Da were watching all this. There was chaos over it. I wasn't allowed take her out again after that.

I was quieter after I came home. I went back to what I'd been doing – but not as regularly. And it was the time when I really started boxing.

I kept knocking at Joey O'Brien's door. For about a year. I had his head done in. If I'd been Joey, I'd have been, 'Here she comes! Quick, quick – pretend we're not in!' But if I really want something, I'm the kind of person who will keep trying and trying. And trying. I was always like that. Sometimes it's good, sometimes it's bad. But I'm an Olympic champion; that's how I got there. I just won't stop. And I kept knocking on Joey's door. They'd have to let girls into the club. There was going to be a stage when they were going to say, 'Ah, she's a melter, this one – let her in.'

Joey kept at the secretary, Paddy Osborne.

'Look, Paddy – you have to let this girl join. Times are changing, we're not in the Stone Age any more. You have to let her join.'

But Paddy was saying, 'We don't have anywhere for her to change,' and other excuses. He brushed it off.

In the meantime, Joey was working in a gym in Finglas, a huge place on the Jamestown Road. He was doing fitness and boxing classes there – he's a fully qualified fitness coach and personal trainer.

He said to me, 'Look, Kellie – if you want to come out and do a couple of sessions, you can.'

'Brilliant. Where is it? When?'

I went out on the bus. It left me in Finglas village, and I walked the rest of the way, up the Jamestown Road – it wasn't very far. Joey did pads with me. He'd hold up the pads and I'd hit them. It was really exciting, because it felt like I was learning something totally new. He showed me what way to hold my hands, how to stand, what a jab was – all the basic stuff.

I went again and again. I began to meet other people who were training and sparring in the gym. I'd watch them getting into the ring, and they'd have a good spar. They'd get back out, and they'd sit on the side of the ring, talking to each other like mates. They'd just been battering each other, and now they were sitting together, chatting. I realized that I didn't have to be angry or to feel malice towards the other boxer if I was going to fight them in the ring. It was all about switching on and off.

So I started to do it. I'd put the headguard on and the gumshield in, and I'd get into the ring and spar – always with boys.

There was a fella called Vernon Carroll – he's a coach now, in Ballymun. He has a son, Jono Carroll, who would eventually challenge for the IBF Junior Lightweight world title. Vernon started bringing Jono up to the gym. Jono was just a bit younger than me. In his first-ever spar, I gave him a bloody nose. He still remembers it.

Joey and myself would go to my Da's friend Martin Lawless's house, in Whitehall. Joey would get us to jog out there, for the fitness. Then we'd have a little training session, Joey, myself and Martin. Martin's wife, Deirdre, would come out too and hit the bag. Or Martin would hold pads for Deirdre.

Martin was my Da's best friend; he loves my Da. He was always trying to talk to me, trying to get me to stay out of trouble. He was helping my Da by helping me. Later on, Martin would become the first person to sponsor me. MLM Construction – €600.

One night Joey was in Corinthians and Paddy turned round to him.

'Joey – you can bring that young one down during the week if you want.'

Joey knocked at my parents' door, to let me know. But I was out. So he said, 'Tell Kellie she's allowed in.'

When I came home, my Ma and Da told me.

'Wha' – what?!'

I was straight out again and legging it around to Joey's.

'Joey! I'm allowed start – I'm allowed start?!'

'Yeah, yeah – you're in on Tuesdays and Thursdays.'

'Ah – that's deadly!'

Joey's a very quiet person but he knew he was delivering great news. I think he was delighted. I'm very grateful to Joey. I wanted to change – I must have wanted to change.

I remember once, I had these terrible chest pains.

'Ah, Ma – I'm in bits, I'm in bits.'

She took me down to Temple Street Children's Hospital. The doctor examined me, then he looked at my Ma.

'She's growing, Mrs Harrington.'

The embarrassment of that – I'll never forget it.

'You'll have to train separate nights, Kellie,' Joey told me.

They didn't want me training with the lads at first, but I

didn't care. I had my foot in the door. I was in – into Corinthians Boxing Club, on Bella Place.

I started on a Tuesday night.

I went up some steps and there was a balcony – and mirrors. I looked over the balcony, down into a boxing ring. It was class. The balcony was semicircular and the boxing bags were around that semicircle, hanging from the ceiling. I was nervous; my stomach was in a knot – I was shaking. But I was really excited. It was what I'd been wanting for ages, and now I was there.

No one in the club – the other men who were training there – seemed to bat an eyelid. No one passed any remarks.

Joey was explaining where my feet should be, and my hands. He was getting me into the right stance, over and over again, making me practise it and practise it and practise it. I loved it – I absolutely loved it. This was exactly what I wanted to do. I wanted to learn. I wanted to learn how to move. I wanted to learn how to defend myself, where my hands should be while I was also moving.

'That's good.'

'Oh my God,' I thought. 'I'm fuckin' good! He thinks I'm good.'

Joey's a quiet, humble person but he's brilliant. The thing is, he wasn't living in Blackrock and he wasn't having some kid from town knocking on his door and saying, 'Are you a boxing coach? I'm trying to get into a boxing club.' He was living in a block of flats, and he was seeing all these kids hanging around. What Joey saw, I think, was someone asking for help. And he didn't refuse – thank God he didn't. He saw what I was doing and he probably thought, 'This is a chance to help this young one to save herself.'

He'd have helped any one of us sitting on that wall, but I was the only one knocking on his door. I was persistent – he saw that.

Joey and Martin saw that I could box. That was there from the beginning – 'She's very, very good. She has a raw talent.' But I didn't really believe it, because it wasn't the right people who were saying it to me. I was hearing it from the club, I was hearing it from Joey, I was hearing it from my Da and his friend. But I was thinking, 'They're saying this to keep me on the straight and narrow.'

I had Katie Taylor plastered all over my bedroom wall, cuttings from the papers, even before I got into Corinthians. I thought she was deadly. It was great to have a role model like Katie. If she hadn't been there, I might not have thought that what I wanted to do was possible.

The more I was at the club and the more they began to see that I was good, the more they seemed to accept me. I was there, in Corinthians, about three months when they started, slowly, to let me train with the boys.

I hated secondary school. I was learning nothing. I had no interest, I didn't enjoy it, and I just couldn't concentrate.

I'd been kept back a year in primary school, in second class. They said I wasn't ready for third class. I often wonder what would have happened if I hadn't been kept back. I was older than the rest of my class in Larkin Community College. I was tall, and I just felt older. Nobody slagged me – I'd have punched the bleedin' heads off them. I was never afraid of a fight; I was always ready to defend myself or my friends. I never did my homework. I was on detention every day, almost literally every day, to do the homework that I hadn't done. And still I wouldn't do it.

I don't really know how I ended up at the Talbot Centre. I think it might have been the school's home liaison teacher, Mr Soffe, who arranged it. He would have been talking with my Ma. It was on Upper Buckingham Street, very near

Corinthians. I had to go up there, and I think my Ma sat in on the first session.

I'm not sure if I ever knew what it was, really, or why I was there; but it was substance abuse counselling. The counsellor's name was Mary Cotter. I'd just be chatting away. I got one-to-one attention, and I liked that. I still see that lady, Mary Cotter – she still walks past my Ma's house. She was great. She was very mellow and relaxed. She wasn't telling me what to do or how I should do it. She kept us occupied; we cooked while we talked. I'm sure I was being assessed, but I enjoyed it.

Larkin Community College didn't know what to do with me, so they came to some arrangement with Youthreach. I was enrolled there, at their centre on North Great George's Street, under Pat Deery; he was the head of the place, the coordinator. That was during second year. I was finished with school. I'm probably wrong on so many different levels, but I feel that Larkin let me down. I might have been bad, but I was still only a kid.

The thing about Youthreach: it wasn't school. It was for people who had left school before finishing. I wasn't getting homework. I didn't have to bring books home. I got up out of bed in the morning and went there, with no work expected, and I left with no work expected. They paid you to go – I think it was €160 a week. If you weren't there, you didn't get paid.

I did CSPE – Civic, Social and Political Education. I did woodwork. And drama – I loved the drama. The teacher, Anto – Anthony Ferns – had little scripts for us to do, to act out. A friend of mine, Ango's sister Esther, was in the Youthreach too.

Anto would say, 'Right, we're going to do something.'

He'd have a script for us.

'Ah – we'll do our own script,' we'd tell him.

We acted out *EastEnders*. We were Kat and Alfie Moon. Anto said it was good. He told me later that if I hadn't made it at boxing I could have been an actress. And, to a certain extent, I feel that I *do* perform when I'm going to box. But I loved pretending to be someone else and not myself. At that time I really didn't know who the fuck I was.

There was singing too. I love singing. We sang 'The Green Fields of France' and 'The Wild Colonial Boy'. Anto entered me into a competition with students from other Youthreach centres and vocational colleges. We went over to the college in Ringsend.

Other students from our Youthreach had come to give me their support, and Anto was there too. The other contestants were getting up and singing traditional Irish folk songs. I was sitting there, sweating, and thinking, 'Ah, Jesus Christ – why did I say I'd come over here?'

I wanted to leave. But Anto wasn't having it.

'No, Kellie – just see how you go.'

So I got up and I sang 'The Wild Colonial Boy' – and I loved it. Then we had to stick around till the end, to see who'd won. And it was me – I'd bleedin' won. I won! I was thinking, 'The judges must've felt sorry for me or something.' But it was like winning *The X Factor*. It was amazing. I was expecting Louis Walsh to sign me up.

There was a bit of a celebration – tea and scones and sponge cake. That was what Youthreach was like, very friendly and warm. In school there'd been no relationship with the teachers. It was just – get in, sit down, learn and get out. But this was very different, and I felt normal.

Eddie Daly was the cookery teacher. I loved those classes with Eddie, because he was a person who listened. He never tried to solve the problem that I might have been talking about, but he listened. I'd have a little rant and he'd be rambling around the kitchen, getting us to cut the onions, crush the garlic, chop the peppers, add the oregano and the tomato puree – open the tin of chopped tomatoes! I'd be doing all that and talking to him. I don't even know if he was listening. He might have been thinking, 'Ah, Jaysis – here she goes again.'

We went out on outdoor activities; Eoin Browne brought us out. Before we left, someone was always in charge of getting the flasks of soup ready, making the sandwiches, getting the packets of King crisps. Leaving the city – it was like leaving the country, even though we were only going to Donabate and Dalkey. We'd go on walks. It felt like we were walking for ever, but it was probably only a kilometre. We'd walk, and stop for our tea and the sandwiches would be handed around. They were always in cling film, so we could see whether they were cheese or ham or ham and cheese. I always got the ham. I'd get my packet of King and I'd crush the crisps and put them into the sandwich, on top of the ham. It was delicious. It could be cold enough, but the soup would warm us. We'd gather up the rubbish and continue on the walk. There was only one bus, and I made sure I was on that bus every week.

I wasn't getting into trouble and I was having fun. And I was learning. If I'd done anything wrong I'd have been kicked out of Youthreach – and I loved Youthreach. I wanted to stay.

Brother Martin Byrne, the English teacher, got us to write stories. It was an exercise where I could just imagine and dream. I wrote a story about how I loved boxing. I was being just me on paper; there was no one standing over me, judging what I was doing. And I wrote about how Katie Taylor was my inspiration, and about how I'd love to box for Ireland. It went into a little book, *Writing on the Wall*. Years later, in 2018, a copy of the book came through the letterbox of my Ma and Da's house. Brother Martin had dropped it in, to say, *Look at where you are now; look at where you were back then.*

My first pair of gloves were given to me by a fella called Mark O'Toole, who's now a coach in a boxing club in Meath. A brand new pair. Everlast. Proper boxing gloves – red. I loved them. I felt like a real boxer. I had them for a long time but the problem is, gloves get smelly. You don't want to get rid of them because the glove moulds into the shape of your hand. But the smell – you just can't take it any more and you have to get a new pair. Sometimes you'll be sparring with someone and they'll give you a smack, and you'd nearly be knocked out by the smell, never mind the smack. The whiff off the glove is disgusting. It's not just the gloves, it's the wraps. You bandage your hands, then you put your hands into the gloves, and your hands sweat, inside this small space – leather keeping the heat and sweat trapped. It's hard to get the inside of the glove to dry. But I loved those first gloves.

I bought my first pair of boots in the National Stadium – the amateur boxing headquarters. They were actually Formula 1 racing driver's boots, but they're sold as boxing boots. I have flat feet, so I'm particular about what boots I wear. These ones were hilarious-looking. And they weighed a ton. They were yellow, and kind of velvety. And I put pink laces in them. I thought they were deadly. I still have them at home.

I liked the routine of binding my hands and putting on the gloves – all of that. They're the simple things that you do in your daily routine. I broke my thumb twice in one year, 2019, coming up to the Olympic Qualifiers. So I have to bandage my hands really well. I tape the bandages, to keep them in place. It's all preparation, for going to war with the bag. I know the bag isn't going to hit me back, but there are coaches watching and they're calling out combinations, with a whistle, or just shouting – they're watching, and it's intense. The bag is swinging and I don't want it swinging too much because I'll be running after it. The bag is an opponent – I'm almost treating it like it's human. It's moving back and forwards, like a human is moving – and to the side. If I hit it hard it's going to move; if I hit it soft, it's not moving. If I go easy on the bag and don't do the shots being called by the coach, I won't be fit. It'll be lazy work. What you put in, you get out. So I like to say, 'Go to war with the bag.'

Sometimes, if I'm having a shit day, I take out my frustration on the bag. I quickly realize how hard boxing is, because – going to war on the bag – I'm exhausted, dead. I stop breathing and I'm leathering the bag out of it. All technique goes out the window. And I'm empty then, I'm drained.

'Jesus Christ, I'm wrecked.'

I was still sitting on the wall at the flats, but not as much. And I'd be hiding from Joey. I was training, but still drinking at the weekends – Friday, Saturday, Sunday. That's a lot if you're in sport. I'd be going to Barcode, in Fairview, and Q Bar, at O'Connell Bridge, and Reds, opposite Q Bar, on Westmoreland Street.

Then I stopped drinking as much and as often, because I was enjoying what I was doing – the boxing – more and more.

From the time I was about sixteen, I was very confused about my sexuality – and not afraid to be openly confused. I didn't care if I kissed a girl or a boy and I didn't care who knew about it.

I told my Ma.

'Ma, I'm gay.'

And she said, 'Yeah – all right, Kellie.'

She just knew me; it wasn't a big deal. We were fighting all the time but I felt comfortable telling my Ma. I'd have been scarlet saying it to my Da; I'd have been mortified. But the next week, after telling her I was gay, I'd be kissing a fella and she'd know about it, because news spreads like wildfire in the inner city.

We called it 'meeting'. Someone would say, 'Here – will you meet me friend?'

'Yeah, right – all right.'

I'd meet him and we'd go for a walk together. Everyone knew, because I was walking around with him. And it got back to my Ma. One week I'm telling her I'm gay and the next I'm walking down the street, holding hands or linking a fella. I'd no idea what was going on with me but I didn't really care who knew.

There were a few girls around the area who were gay, and they were out. It was the same thing, though. I'd kiss them but then they wouldn't hear from me for six months.

Before I could fight I had to have a medical examination. It cost €50, because you couldn't get it on your medical card. Female boxers had a pink card that had to be filled in, and the lads had a blue one. So, off I went to the doctor – eye test, heartbeat checked, weight – and out I came. The doctor already knew that I didn't have a weak heart or epilepsy.

'My Ma's going to kill me. I was only in there for two minutes. She's not getting her money's worth.'

I had my boxing medical card. And now I could get my boxing fight card, where my fights would be recorded. I was now a carded boxer.

Paddy Osborne got me a fight after about three months, my first fight, against a girl who'd been boxing for about three years. It was me and just one other girl, Debbie Rogers, on the team, with a bunch of men and boys, on the bus to Cavan. Debbie was boxing for Westside Boxing Club, in Tallaght, and it was her coach from Westside, Billy Stacey, who was our coach, in our corner, for the night.

So I'm in the ring, my first fight ever. My nerves are absolutely gone. I hit the girl, Caroline O'Reilly, and I go, 'Oh – sorry, sorry!'

And she was a brute. I was like, 'Oh my God—!' She hit me real hard. I'll never forget it – she milled me out of it. I was trying to give it back; I was trying to box. There were three rounds in the fight, two minutes each round. In the last round, with about ten seconds to go, the referee stopped the fight, because I was getting battered. He could have stopped it earlier and declared her the winner, but he let it go on and then he stopped it ten seconds before the end. That was the worst bit. It was a stoppage.

I was raging. I cried the whole way home.

There were people on the bus, excited and happy because they'd won and they had their little trophies, but I wasn't in any mood to be smiling. I remember sitting there, sniffling, with the tears running down my face. I was sitting beside Debbie.

'I'm going to fight her again.'

'Yeah, yeah – you will an' all.'

'I'm going to come back and beat her.'

I thought I knew why I'd been put into that situation – the reason why some of the men in the boxing club had put me in against a girl with much more experience: 'We'll get rid of her now.' It was never said, but that was what I felt. They were testing me.

'We'll see – does she really want it or not.'

4

'What's your name?'
'Kellie Harrington.'
'There is no Kellie – it's Recruit Harrington!'

It's all about your stance and where your feet should be. If you're right-handed, your left leg and left hand are forward. You're using your left hand as your jab hand. Your left hand is your good hand but your right hand is your *great* hand. You lead with your left. You're keeping the other fighter at bay, keeping them away from you. But you're setting them up for the big one, the right.

Your hips are slightly turned, so you're not square on to your opponent. Being side on makes it a lot harder for your opponent to land shots. Square on, you're a bigger target, and your balance isn't great. Side on, the heel of the back foot comes up just slightly off the ground; you're nice and light on your feet. Your knees are slightly bent and your shoulders are dropped and relaxed; your elbows stay in, your hand stays closed, in a fist; your thumb comes out across your knuckles. Your chin stays down – you still stay nice and relaxed.

Moving forward, moving back, moving forward, moving back, then moving side to side – how you stand and how you keep your shape. Your right hand should be at the side of your chin and your lead hand should be up, just underneath the eyeline.

I start to bring in punches. Go forward and throw a jab, come back and throw a jab. Go forward and throw a one-two, come back and throw a one-two. Go to the side and throw a jab, go to the side and throw a one-two. Go to the other side and throw a right hand; go to the other side and throw a jab. Again and again, and again.

I started sparring with the lads. I loved it, because they wouldn't take it easy on me. They showed respect by making me work hard; they never stood and took shots just because I was a woman. There was one fella, Shane Roche. He was a year or two younger than me, and smaller. But he was class. He was a mini Mike Tyson, coming forward, throwing loads of punches. When I was fit, I'd get the better of him, because I was tall and had the longer reach than him; I was able to keep him at a distance. I'd be panting, but the adrenaline would keep me on my toes, keep me fast and light. The nerves would be going. But nerves are good, because they make you feel alive – which makes you move.

If I was landing nice shots on him he wouldn't stop to look out of the ring, because I'd catch him again if he did. But I could see his eyes move; he was checking to see if any-one had seen that he was after getting hit by a girl.

He dropped me a few times, with body shots. I'd get tired and the feet would slow down, and that was when Mike Tyson came in – he's moving, he's bobbing, he's weaving from side to side; he rolls in, throws a left into the body and a right into the body, rolls back out, throws another left – *boomp!* Down I go, and he steps back.

'Ah, Jesus Christ – I'm in a jocker here.'

I have a knee on the floor.

'Right – that's me done now.'

I'm doubled up, in pain, like someone has just pulled my

insides out. I'm winded, gasping. I'm not thinking of anything, except the pain.

Then the emotional pain kicks in.

'Fuckin' hell, I'm after getting dropped there. I'm a gobshite – I need to get fitter. I need to stay on my toes more.'

I'd have to make sure it didn't happen the next time. I was good at keeping it long, keeping him off, with the length – my reach – with the movement, with my boxing craft. But if I wasn't fit and he got in on the inside, then I was in trouble. If I lost focus, that was it; he was in and – *boomp, boomp, boomp* – he was getting the shots off.

You suck it up and get back in.

It wasn't a tournament fight and the result wasn't going to go on my card, but I really wanted to beat this girl, Caroline O'Reilly, the girl who'd beaten me in Cavan the year before. This time, the fight was in Corinthians. I was cold, but sweating too, because I was nervous and anxious.

It was a completely different fight. I didn't batter her or anything; it was a good, close fight. But I was so happy that I was actually able to box and that I wasn't saying 'Sorry' every time I hit her. There was more skill in it this time, and I moved my head out of the way of her punches instead of standing there and eating them. It felt different.

My hand was lifted – I was the winner. I was delighted with myself. It felt like I'd won a World Championship. It was absolutely amazing.

I say it to Paddy Osborne, today.

'You didn't get rid of me that easy, did you?'

He knows I'm joking and he laughs.

The IABA – the amateur boxing association – ran little tournaments for girls. Anja Norman was the IABA's Women's

Development Officer. She'd been brought in from Sweden in 2006, as part of the Women in Sport initiative. Her job was to get more women involved in boxing. She organized the national squad training, and camps for women. She was brilliant, but I don't think she ever had enough influence. There were other people pulling her back, thinking that she was getting too big for her boots, doing too much.

The tournaments she organized weren't formal championships; they were just fights. But they were in the National Stadium. They'd pick a selection of female boxers from around the country and the invitations went out to the clubs. You could be in against someone really good one week and fighting someone with no real experience the next. There'd be girls fighting each other at different weights – not massive differences, a kilo or two – to give us more ring experience.

I was training at Corinthians, getting to know everybody, starting to build up relationships with the people in the club. When a tournament was coming up – say, the Dublin Leagues or the Under-18s or the Youth Championships – the boxers involved would be getting more pad work, more sparring work. The coaches would be watching them a little bit more, making sure that they were staying sharp – keeping their hands up, moving their feet the right way, not falling asleep at the bags. I was going into these little competitions, so I was getting more attention from the coaches. I wasn't just boxing for myself; I was boxing for the club. The coaches wanted me to do well for the club, but they also wanted me to do well for myself. They didn't want me to get hurt, and they didn't want to send in someone who didn't know what she was doing. I'd be looked after that bit more; I got special treatment coming closer to fights. There'd be a great buzz in the club the night before the weigh-in, usually a Thursday night. Everyone would be saying, 'Best of luck tomorrow, Kellie.' I'd be feeling great, leaving the club.

I'd have an extra layer of clothes on, to make me sweat a bit more, get the weight down. I wouldn't eat or drink then, until after the weigh-in. I was boxing at 63 kilos at the time.

I'd go home and get my bag ready for the next day – my gumshield, a red kit and a blue kit, because I didn't know which corner, red or blue, I was going to be in. 'Corinthians Boxing Club' was printed on the back of the vests. Someone once gave me pink shorts and a pink vest with my name on it, but I never wore them. I've no objection to pink but I'd have been scarlet boxing in that kit. People would be going, 'What the fuck is that? Is she trying to tell us something or wha'?'

I loved the Corinthians kit because I felt that I was representing the club family. I'd always get excited wearing the kit. I feel the same way today when I wear my St Mary's kit. The kit was always big on me – it was swinging off me. No matter what kit I had, it was always big. Sometimes I'd have to tape the straps at the back of the vest.

I'd put my boxing gloves into the bag, for pad work before the fight. You don't wear your own gloves in a tournament fight, because you could have put a horseshoe into one of them! You're given gloves for the fight.

I'd always get a lift to the National Stadium for the weigh-in. Walking in, I'd be freezing *and* sweating – cold sweats – very nervous but kind of thrilled. Being in the National Stadium – knowing that I'd be boxing there – was amazing. There'd be people there who knew one another and at first I felt a bit alone, left out. But Anna Moore and Sadie Duffy, the two ladies in charge of the weigh-ins, were absolutely lovely. They'd have their list of the girls who were competing. Dervla Duffy, from Castleblayney – she was a jockey as well

43

as a boxer; Ceire Smith, from Cavan; Moira McElligott, from Kerry – she was a jockey too; Laura O'Neill, from St Paul's Boxing Club in Kilkenny; Shanice Juste, from Arklow; Lynne O'Shea – she's coaching now, in St Paul's, in Waterford. I remember fighting Deirdre Walsh, from Athy, and Laura McHale – but not on the same night! Laura was from the same club as Deirdre, St Michael's, Athy.

Sinéad Kavanagh was always there. Sinéad boxed with Peter Perry in CIE Boxing Club, in Inchicore. I'd go over to the club and spar with her, and she'd come over to my club. Sinéad was 75 kilos, and a little bit taller than me. She moved to Drimnagh Boxing Club, with Tony Davitt. I'd spar with her there, nearly every Saturday. They call her Sinéad 'KO' Kavanagh, because she's a banger; she loves to have a scrap. That's exactly what it was every Saturday; we'd just kill each other. And that's how we became the best of pals.

Winning is much more important to me now than it was back then. Being part of something, just being involved, was what mattered to me. It was about being there, taking part, making friends, building relationships with coaches and other people in the club. The hunger to win came later, when I began to realize that I was decent and the confidence started to come. I could win fights and I could look forward to winning.

I'd get my kit on in the changing room. I didn't have a gown. Even today, I'd never wear one. I'd be worried that I'd put it on, then go and get the head slapped off me. 'She had a gown on her an' all, and she still got battered.'

I'd come out of the dressing room and I'd tell the coach, 'I'm ready.' Sometimes they opened the doors of the Ring-side Club for us. Normally the Ringside is used as a bar, for Senior Championships or for concerts, but we'd be allowed to warm up in there. All the chairs and tables would have been put away, so there'd be a big floor for us.

The coach would be walking up the steps, to see what fight was on. There might be eight fights on the card; the coach would be checking to see who was in the ring. There'd have been four fights an hour; if I was in the eighth fight and the fourth was still on, there was an hour to go before my fight. The coach would tell me to take my time, and loosen out, do a bit of stretching. He'd be keeping me calm and focused.

When it came to the fight before mine, I'd be as nervous as anything – the adrenaline pumping, my heart coming through my chest. I'd be listening out for the bell – the ding announcing the final round of the fight before mine.

The bell goes.

'Shit – I'm nearly ready to go.'

I have to start walking towards the ring. I'm walking up the steps. The girl I'll be fighting is right beside me. Up, then down more steps. I'm at the ring. I'm standing at the red corner, waiting for the girl who was in the previous fight to come down from the ring. We touch each other's gloves.

'Good luck.'

'Well done.'

The ring announcer is calling out the judges' names, and whatever side of the ring they're sitting.

'And your referee will be – Sadie Duffy.'

Once Sadie is in the ring and my name is called, it's time for me to step in. I'm going up the steps – I'm shaking.

I walk to the middle of the ring. I turn around. I kick my feet, I flick them backwards, three times. I walk back to my corner. I bang my gloves in front of me, I bang them behind my back, I bang them to the front again. I tip the corner of the ring, then I punch my coach's hand. I bless myself and say, 'Look after me,' to my Nanny and my Grandda.

That's my routine. When I go into the centre of the ring,

I'm saying it's mine – 'I don't give a fuck, this is my happy place' – even though I'm terrified. I'm forcing myself to become the predator – I own the ring.

I fought Natasha Lynch in November 2006. It was my first proper carded fight. I won that one. She kept coming forward. She was very aggressive, but it wasn't planned aggression. And that was great because I was able to catch her all the time. I was picking up the points, and I beat her well.

Back then, the way the pointing system worked, when I caught her with the jab, say, the point would go up on the screen. The points accumulated throughout the fight. I wouldn't look at the screen while I was boxing but I'd hear people in the crowd.

'Ah, ref – she's fuckin' hit her there – the points aren't going up!'

I could tell how I was doing by the shouts.

I'd expected to win but I was still nervous getting into the ring; my stomach was going, I was shaking. But I love that; I embrace it. I'm so nervous, but I feel alive. I come out of myself; I'm a different person. When I'm in the ring, people might look at me and think, 'She's a cocky bitch.' People *have* said it of me. Sometimes I'd bring my hands down, taunting, daring the other boxer to come at me. I wouldn't really be aware of it. I wasn't showing off – I was alive!

I'd always had this vision – since I was small – of me being in the Army. I thought it was something that I'd be good at, and that Army life would suit me. They wouldn't take me until I was eighteen. So I was waiting. Then, when I turned eighteen I sent in the application; the career guidance teacher in Youthreach helped me with it.

I got the call to go for the fitness test, which took place in the Phoenix Park. I had to run a mile and a half, and I think I had fourteen minutes to do it. The men had to do it in less time. I was fit enough from boxing, so I did the run and had plenty of time left over. There were press-ups and sit-ups, twenty of each in a minute – easy peasy.

I went for the medical in St Bricin's Military Hospital, in Arbour Hill. I got everything done – blood, heart, the works. I took off my shoes and they checked my feet. And I failed the medical: I had flat feet.

I was like, 'What – the – fuck.'

I was bawling my eyes out.

I *do* have flat feet, but I'd no idea back then. I didn't know what flat feet were.

So I said, 'That's discrimination.'

I didn't know what else to say. Then I tried something else: 'I want a second opinion.'

So I was given a second go and this time I curled my feet up a little bit to the side – made a curve – so they wouldn't be so flat. What happens is, they wet your feet and get you to walk across a blue surface, to leave an imprint. So I was walking along, making an arch on each foot. And they were like, 'Her feet are brand new!'

That was it – I'd passed.

A few weeks later I got the summons in the door. I was due to commence my recruit training in Gormanston Military Camp, in Meath. I had to get black activewear – tops, shorts and leggings – pyjamas, socks, underwear, and black polish for my boots. I was looking forward to it, but nervous too. I'd had this vision of myself in the Army, but in reality I had no idea what I'd signed up for.

I can't remember who gave me the lift to the barracks but I do remember being dropped there. I had my sports bag, with everything in it. There were other people arriving, and everyone looked nervous. There was a chill in the air. The minute we arrived, the corporals came out and they were all shouting at us.

'Stand there! Stand there!'

I was looking back at them but one of them roared.

'Don't fuckin' eyeball *me*!'

I was thinking, 'Oh, Jesus Christ – what's he mean, "eyeball me"? Where am I meant to look?'

'What's your name?'

'Kellie Harrington.'

'There is no Kellie – it's Recruit Harrington!'

All the shouting – these men could kill you with their voices.

'This is your new life now!'

I was looking around to see if I knew anybody else there. And I did. Daniel Downey – Dano – from Portland Place, not far from where I lived. I felt a bit better now, because I knew someone.

I'd had this picture of what the barracks was going to be like, almost like a small town. But the reality was far from what I'd imagined. It was very eerie, and cold. There was a haunted, ghostly feeling off it. My dorm was *so* empty, and old. The bathrooms were echoey; I imagined I was hearing things. There was only one other girl who started with me, Stephanie Doyle. It was just me and her in this massive dormitory, the whole floor.

We could hear all the lads upstairs, with their radios on, the tunes pumping, having the craic, and it was just me and Stephanie downstairs. And she left after a month. Another girl came in, Amy Crooke. But I was left in the dorm on my own quite a lot of the time, because Amy was in a different platoon.

*

We did the basic drilling, marching over and over again.

'Left, left – left, right, left.'

Stop, turn, stand to attention; stand at ease, stand to attention, get ready to march – march.

We were shown our first rifle, a Steyr AUG, and were given a manual – instructions about how it worked, and how to clean it, how to assemble it. It was like being back in school; half of the details never went into my head. We learnt how to strip it, how to put it together, how to clean the barrel, how to fill the magazine. The bullets were blanks but you had to make sure that every single bullet was accounted for.

It was nerve-racking, but good. I was always a bit worried that I'd lose a blank or the gun would go off accidentally. We had to sign out our rifles and when we got to the rifle range, the CQ – the Company Quartermaster Sergeant – gave us our rounds. When we were finished, we had to clean the rifles and declare that we had no ammunition left, before heading back to the barracks and signing the rifles back in. I'm not sure that I ever hit a target. But I must have hit something, because they were letting me carry on with the training.

We were taken up to McKee Barracks, in Cabra, to be measured for our uniforms. The boots were terrible – flat and uncomfortable. I was already thinking that I'd buy myself a pair of good boots in Army Bargains, on Little Britain Street. But I loved wearing the uniform. Every time I went out on parade I felt really proud.

There was a buddy system in place from the very beginning, and Daniel Downey was my buddy. If I turned up on parade and there wasn't a nice crease in my uniform trousers – we used to starch them – or if my boots weren't polished properly, then Dano would be in trouble. He'd be made to dance or sing in front of the platoon. But Dano didn't give a shite, because he liked dancing and singing and he didn't lack confidence.

Some of the things that brought trouble down on us were mad. A thread hanging from the insignia on your sleeve – that got you into trouble.

'Right, everybody – into your civvies!'

'Civvies' was our training gear. They'd make us run to the tower of the old aerodrome – we called the tower the Mushroom – and back. But, actually, myself and Dano didn't get into a whole lot of trouble. It was a real comfort to have him there.

We had to do a 10K jog once or twice a week. Gormanston is near the sea, and we'd run down onto the beach. We'd be going along and Corporal Dunne would shout:

'Ice cream!'

And we had to shout back:

'You scream!'

'We all scream!'

'For ice cream!'

He'd shout:

'Who wants ice cream?!'

Meaning, who wants to get into the water. No one would answer him, and he'd make us all run down into the sea. We'd be frozen.

The training was absolutely mad. It was tough, mentally very, very tough. The grub was great, though. It's all about the food! The chef was a boxing coach. Trigger – he's a coach in Edenmore. I didn't know him then, but he knew I boxed. He was always nice to me. I'd be hungry, because I was living on my nerves; I really found it tough. You never knew when they were going to shout, 'Get on parade!', 'You're going for ice cream!', 'You're going out to the Mushroom!', 'Drop down – hit the deck and leopard crawl!' – you had to use your elbows to crawl. I'd be starving at the end of every day.

One of the corporals would call, 'Get on parade!', and

everyone would have to go around – get on parade – making sure we were all awake. If it was the middle of the night, it was up to us to make sure that we were all up out of bed and that no one was left behind.

'We're on parade now, we're on parade now!'

I walk and talk in my sleep; I always have. I was sleepwalking one night, and I ran out onto the stairs. I'd put my shirt on and my boots, and I was shouting.

'Everybody on parade, everybody on parade!'

Corporal Keenan was out, after me.

'What the fuck is going on?! Harrington?!'

I was like, 'Huh?'

'Get the fuck back in now!'

He pulled me the next morning.

'Harrington, what's going on?'

He explained to me what had happened. I'd been asleep. He said, 'Maybe you should go and see the doctor.'

I did that, and the doctor prescribed sleeping tablets. But I didn't take them. Sleepwalking is just what I do. It's part of my make-up. If I'm stressed, it's much worse. Coming up to a fight, you'll get a better conversation out of me when I'm asleep than you will during the day.

We got out on the weekends, and I'd just go on the piss for the whole weekend with the other recruits – Kavo, Mooney, Dano. It was a good platoon; they were all sound. Friday night, Saturday, then we'd be back to the barracks on Sunday. That became the routine after about three weeks.

You pass out as a two-star private after four months of training. Before that, you do a week in the Glen of Imaal, in the Wicklow Mountains. Scratch training. It was a week but it felt like a month. I don't know how I got through it. We dug a trench – it was just a hole in the ground – and stayed in it for twenty-four hours. We had to pretend that we were under fire, in a war situation, but I was just firing into the air. I can't even remember if I had infrared goggles. I had no real idea of what I was doing. If it had been actual combat, I'd have been blown off the face of the earth.

'Let off your rounds – fire back!'

I was lying back in the trench, firing into the sky. I couldn't see a thing. I didn't know who was who around me; we all had camouflage make-up on – and it was pitch black.

I was supposed to shoot at a target but I couldn't see it; I didn't know what I was shooting at. I was going through rivers that smelt like cow shit. It was just hell. We weren't allowed to get our rifles dirty – but it was impossible to keep them clean, because we were going through muck all day. We'd have to clean the rifle at night. The corporals and sergeants would come around, to check. If your rifle wasn't clean, you got the rest of the platoon in the shit. You were constantly on edge.

'Ah, Jesus – I hope this is clean enough.'

I wanted to leave. I couldn't see further than the week in the Glen.

'This is my life?! Get me bleedin' out of here!'

Really, that's not what the Army is all about. It was just a week in the training, to make you or break you. And it broke me.

I called the corporal and I said, 'I want my ticket' – meaning, I wanted out.

They couldn't believe it because, to them, it hadn't looked like I was struggling. But I was.

The corporal said, 'Harrington – get back to your platoon and finish it out.'

But I came back: 'I want me ticket.'

The sergeant came over and had a word with me.

'Listen,' he said. 'We'll put you in the kitchen for a few hours.'

They sent me into the camp kitchen so the people in there, the chefs, could talk me out of it. I was sitting in there, and they were like, 'You've done so well.'

They were very persuasive, very motivational.

'You've nearly done it – you've a day and a half left. What would you be going for? You're nearly there. You'd be mad if you stopped now.'

I was like, 'Ah, no – I can't do this.'

'This isn't what it's like – once you pass out, it's different.'

So I went, 'Fuck it – I'll stay.'

I stayed and I did it; I finished the training.

The last thing we had to do was walk out of the Glen, back to the trucks. It wasn't particularly far, but I felt like I'd been walking for days; I was broke up. I had all my gear and I think I was carrying a GPMG – a general-purpose machine gun – as well.

A jeep came up beside me.

'Put your hand on the wing mirror there.'

They were giving me a boost, to help me along. The jeep was a walking stick. They couldn't give me a lift, so I soldiered on out.

When we got to the trucks, there was more hanging around. Everyone was anxious.

'This isn't the end – they're just letting us think it's the end.'

'They're going to make us march back in there again.'

But, thankfully, it *was* the end.

We got back to the barracks and we had unarmed combat. There were no other girls, so I had to fight one of the lads. I got stuck in and it was brilliant; I was delighted doing it. There were no rules; it was kill or be killed. Not literally – there was no bad killing! But the rules were pretty basic – don't gouge anyone's eyes out. It was basically having a scrap. I'd happily fight all day, without weapons. But give me a gun and I'll be going, 'Ah, Jesus – what do I do with this?'

I did really well at the unarmed combat. I was definitely having second thoughts about leaving. There were only three months to go before I'd pass out as a private three-star.

I was the only woman in the platoon. I never got a hard time because of that. But I was alone. The lads were up the stairs, on their lines – that's the dormitory. If I went upstairs, I had to shout, 'Female on the lines,' in case any of them were indecent. If a corporal was coming down to my floor, he'd have to shout, 'Male on the lines!'

When he walked in I'd have to stand at attention.

He'd say, 'At ease,' and I could relax.

One night, I was upstairs polishing my boots with the lads, when the Company Quartermaster Sergeant came in. We stood up to attention – but there was murder, because I was there.

He was raging.

'What are you doing up here? You shouldn't be here – you're a female!'

It pissed me off, because my corporal had told me, 'Look, Harrington – you're the only woman. You're allowed up onto the male lines, just shout, "Female on the lines!" before you go in and you're fine – as long as you shout that.'

So I told the Quartermaster Sergeant that I'd cleared it with the corporal and that I was allowed up there.

But I think it was the final push. He'd made me feel really bad about myself.

I was thinking, 'D'you know what – fuck this shit.'

The man who was giving out to me was the same man who'd tried to talk me out of leaving. It just made my mind up for me. I was lonely downstairs, by myself. I'd too much time to think.

I went home at the weekend and I said to my parents, 'I don't know whether I want this.'

But I didn't want to be a failure. If I left, what was I going to do with the rest of my life? I didn't want to be there but I felt like I'd be letting them down. The Army was a good job. I thought the pay was good.

But my Ma and Da were great.

'Look, Kellie – it's your decision. Don't be thinking about anybody else. If you want to stay, stay. If you want to leave, leave. But be happy with the decision.'

I'd wanted them to make my mind up for me, but they were right.

I went back to the barracks after the weekend, and I saw the corporal, Corporal Keenan. He was involved in boxing too. I told him that I wanted to leave.

I was getting a name in boxing. I'd even been given a week off, four or five days, to box, when I was doing the recruit training, and that – the time off – was unheard of; I knew that.

It was the first ever all-female international boxing tournament in Ireland, and I was in Ireland's first full female team. Ireland against England, in Dungarvan, in Waterford. Gerry O'Mahony, from Dungarvan Boxing Club, put the show together, with Pete Taylor and Pat Ryan.

Katie Taylor was there. Being on the same team as someone I looked up to and admired; it was amazing to think that I was there and that I was boxing on the same show. She was phenomenal.

'Oh my God – I'm on the same bill as a World champion.'

I was good enough to be on the same team as her. I was half-decent.

My old foe, Caroline O'Reilly from Cavan, was on the team too. My friend Sinéad Kavanagh was there; also Olga

Conroy from Dungarvan, and Marsha Halpin from Drimnagh. I'd boxed Marsha in the National Stadium, and she'd beaten me by a point. Alana Murphy from Eastside Boxing Club in Belfast was there, and Christina McMahon, from Castleblayney. And Clara Fraher from Dungarvan – Clara was one of my first proper boxing friends.

Katie fought at 63 kilos against Amanda Coulson, who's now a coach with the England team. Savannah Marshall was on the England team as well. She's the WBO middleweight champion now.

I was boxing at 60 kilos. I was probably 61 kilos, but they give you a 1-kilo allowance when you're boxing in a show like that. I boxed Michelle Smith, and it was tough. She was older than me, more experienced – probably the age I am now. And she was in some nick.

'Oh my God – look at the muscles on her, she's going to bleedin' kill me.'

But I know now: the bigger they are, the harder they fall. I won! I beat her on points. It was absolutely brilliant.

It was great being part of the women's team – part of history. Beating England 6–2, in Ireland. We'd sent them packing. It was a great experience, being there, fighting, watching everybody else, cheering on my teammates.

Two days before the tournament, the IABA had decided that it couldn't be billed as a full international. But we wore the Irish crest on our kit anyway and, after we'd won, the authorities changed their minds and it went on record as a full international.

I think I first met Clara in Coleraine. Anja Norman had put together a training camp for female boxers. Clara was there, and Sinéad and Katie. The coaches were Pete Taylor and Pat Ryan. Clara and me became friends. I used to go down to her house, in Dungarvan; I'd stay down there for the weekend.

Her Ma and Da are absolute legends. They had quads and scramblers, and we'd go on the quads with Clara's uncle, Willie, and her brother, Christopher, and her sister, Cassie. I felt like part of the family when I was there. Clara would come up to Dublin and stay with me. And every time she stayed my clothes would go missing. I'd be looking all around for them and the next time I'd see her she'd be wearing them.

'Ah – that's where they went.'

She still says today, 'I'll be up next week – have you any nice clothes?'

One time, Dungarvan Boxing Club were having a show, and there was no one to match Clara with, so I said I'd go down to Dungarvan and do it. But it wasn't the most hotly contested fight ever.

The referee, Larry Durand, stopped the fight and he said to me, 'Do you know her?'

'Yeah.'

He turned to Clara.

'Do you know *her*?'

'Yeah.'

'Well, yis have to box,' he said. 'Yis have to hit each other.'

And I went, 'But I'm staying in her house later on.'

He burst out laughing.

I boxed Clara after that, in 2009, in the Under-21 Championships, in the National Stadium. That's what I love about boxing. You can make friends and still get in there and box, and remain friends – the fight is over.

Corporal Keenan really wanted me to stay.

'Stick it out, Harrington,' he advised me. 'You'll go very, very far with boxing in the Army. You won't even have to work! You'll just box – that's it.'

'Ah, no – I want out.'

I'd never heard of anyone boxing for the Army.

The sergeant had the same talk with me. But I'd made my decision.

They brought me to the Company Quartermaster Sergeant and he sat me down.

'You know, you'll have a great life in the Army. You're practically finished with the hard part. You've only three months left and you'll be a private three-star. You'll go to the World Championships – you'll just box for the Army. You'll be the face of the Irish Army's boxing team.'

The man who was trying to talk me out of leaving was the same man who'd bawled me out of it for being a female on the men's lines.

I was like, 'Yeah – no – I want out.'

I couldn't see past the three months that were left; I couldn't see life after that. If I'd stayed longer, I'd have had to pay my way out – not a whole lot, but I just wanted out. If I'd been older I might have seen it differently. But I was eighteen, and three months were like three years.

It would have been different if there'd been more females there. There *were* women applying – I know that. So why weren't they there? When I did the fitness test, there were other women there and they were passing too. I remember talking to some of them. It felt like it had been set up that way, to *not* let the women through. I felt alone. If there'd been more women together – instead of a few in each platoon – we could have pushed each other on in training, supported one another. There were forty-two men and two women at the start of my training – and there were a lot more than two women who wanted to join the Army. I'd have been happier if I'd been training with more women.

I left – I was out.

*

I tried to get back into the Army years later, when I was twenty-five. It felt like I had unfinished business. I wanted to do the full training, to get through it, and to prove to myself that I was more mature. But by then they'd introduced an aptitude test – a written exam. I think I went to the National Basketball Arena in Tallaght to do it. But I didn't get a high enough score; it was like looking at a different language. I tried again – the same story. It was online this time, but I still couldn't figure most of it out. I got a friend of mine who I thought would be good at it to have a go, but he couldn't get through it either.

'Ah here, Kellie – it *is* rocket science!'

'D'you know what?' I said to myself. 'What's meant for you won't pass you by, and what passes you by obviously wasn't meant for you. That's it, Kellie – that chapter's closed.'

But I'd still love to do it, just to prove that I can. I'd give it a good bash. I wouldn't be afraid – because I was terrified back then that I'd keep making mistakes. I'd just love to do the training. I wouldn't be afraid now.

5

I have that staying power because of where I'm
from, Dublin's inner city. I don't give a shit – I
don't care what others think.

I was training in Corinthians from Monday to Friday. I could
go down on the nights when there wasn't formal training and
do pads with Joe or Paddy Corcoran, if I wanted to. But I
didn't want to be going into the club on Mondays, feeling
half-dead and getting dropped by body shots from Shane
Roche because I'd been out on the tear over the weekend.

If I was to drink now, today, and I lost a fight two months
from now, I'd blame that loss on the drink. One session can
set you back weeks. I was learning this from experience. I
was being told, too, but I had to learn it for myself.

I loved the training and I very rarely missed it. The club
had installed a women's changing room. It was very small –
you could only have fitted two women into it – but it had a
shower, and a toilet.

If I couldn't get a spar in Corinthians I'd go up to Phibsborough, to the club there. Richard Fox and Terry Hamilton
were the coaches. I'd train there, and sometimes I'd get sparring sessions. A kick-boxing club used the gym too, and a girl
called Barbara Delaney was in that club. She was a lot smaller
than me but she was tough. I could have hit that woman with
the stool from the corner of the ring and she'd have kept
coming at me. I'd spar with her, and it would always be a war.

Shots would be thrown and I'd hear 'Oooh!' and 'Oh!' from outside the ring – everyone was watching. But it was great. It was good for her, because she might be kick-boxing with girls who'd be a lot taller than her. And it was good for me because I was nearly always the taller one in my fights, so it made sense to be sparring with a smaller woman. And she just never stopped. No matter what I hit her with, she was constantly putting pressure on, constantly coming forward and – emotionally – taking bits out of me. When you're hitting someone and it isn't having an effect on them, you know you're in for a rough night.

When I'm in a competition, in the ring, I'm fighting. But to practise what I'm going to do in the ring, I need to spar. It's rehearsing. I'm matched with different sparring partners, with different styles. Shane Roche was shorter than me, with a tight guard that made it difficult to get punches through. He bobbed and weaved like Mike Tyson. He kept coming forward all the time. The only time I could catch him was if I got him to throw, and I could counter at the same time that he was throwing. I'd try to lure him into thinking that I was going to do something, to make him think that he could throw a punch, and I'd counter that, and move.

Then there are the long-range boxers who keep a distance. They might not be as busy; they mightn't have the work rate of a more aggressive boxer like Shane. They choose their punches, and keep it at arm's length; they don't get inside, too close. They'd be a little bit more technical. I need to spar with them too.

There's no winner or loser in sparring; there's nothing on the line. Some people think that's great, and they go all out. They're not afraid of getting caught and they're not afraid of losing. So you can get hurt when you're sparring. I don't spar very well. I box much better than I spar. It's not that I don't push myself, but with nothing on the line the adrenaline isn't kicking in; I'm not pumped. When it comes to a fight, it's different. I know there are judges sitting around the ring, tapping their fingers on the red and blue buttons: 'Red's winning . . . blue's winning . . . red landed . . . blue landed.' I'm sharper, edgier, nervous when I'm fighting. Nerves give me more energy, and I love that.

But I need to spar. I would never go near a tournament if I hadn't sparred before it. It's vital preparation. My speed comes on, I get sharper, and my reactions and distance management improve. Throwing shots at someone who's too far away is pointless, so sparring helps me to close down my distance. I can slip a jab and come back straight away with my right hand. They throw their jab and, if it's their left hand, I come back straight away with my right and I land it, eight times out of ten.

I love sparring with new people, because it's always a fresh challenge. I switch off when I'm sparring with someone I know too well. But if I'm not sparring, I'm not getting that real practice. I can do pads with my coach but it's completely different. I can hit pads all day; you can look like a World champion on pads. Get into the ring, though, and it's a different story.

When I was starting out, I didn't have much difficulty finding boxers to spar with me. There were loads of boys in Corinthians, or I'd go to Drimnagh Boxing Club, Crumlin Boxing Club, or out to Tallaght, to St Mary's, which is my club now.

One time, I went out to Monkstown Boxing Club. At that time, Monkstown had something like sixty girls training there. The club was in a block of flats and it looked as if the wall between two separate flats had been knocked down, to make the space for the club. Maybe the members just said, 'Fuck it – this is our club now,' and went at the walls with sledgehammers, to make the space.

I walked up these steps, into the flats – the club. There were bags hanging everywhere, and pigeons flying across the room, shitting all over the place. I was warming up, ducking to avoid the pigeons, and people belting away on the bags, pigeon feathers floating around in the air. It was chaotic; it was brilliant.

Pauly Kinsella was the coach – he still is.

'Right, Kellie – are you ready? You're sparring with Emer.'

'Yeah, yeah – where are we going?'

'Just into that ring there.'

A regulation ring is about six metres square. This ring was about two metres square. It was tiny. I got in and started to spar with your one, Emer. She cracked me with the inside of her hand, the palm. She'd tried to throw a hook but she slapped me, and that's not allowed. It had been a good spar up to that, but she nearly broke my jaw – I felt the crack.

'My God – what's that?'

The pain of it – the headguard swung around my head. I kept sparring but my leg kept slipping out of the ring, because the ring was so small.

It was absolutely brilliant – the pigeons, the ring, the whole thing; an amazing experience.

I boxed outside Ireland for the first in June 2008, when I fought Natasha Jonas in Liverpool. It was Ireland versus a selection of Liverpool boxers. I'd seen Natasha Jonas fight for England in Dungarvan the year before, so I knew who she was. She was about five years older than me, so she'd had more fights. But I wasn't all that nervous. I was happy to be getting a fight, and the experience. It was very, very tough, pretty much from bell to bell. There was no let-up; a lot of punches thrown, a lot of shots landed. It was punch for punch – it was fuckin' deadly. Boxing matches were divided into four two-minute rounds back then. Two minutes can go very fast, but not in the boxing ring. When you have some-one throwing everything at you, two minutes is a long time. I remember thinking, 'Fuckin' hell,' because she banged – she *hit*. During the last round, I was thinking, 'Oh my God – when is this bell going to go?'

It was very tight. I could have got the nod, but you'll never get the nod on someone else's home turf. I was buzzing after it, even though I didn't get the decision. I remember feeling physically wrecked. There was a lot of hype around Natasha Jonas; she was the one to watch out for. But I was happy that I'd been able to hold my own; I thought I'd done well. It wasn't an important fight but I felt that I'd gained a lot of experience.

A lot of the exhibition fights, fights that haven't been put on my card, have been top class. They're great experiences – literally that, experiences, and preparation for the Europeans and the other big championships.

A month later, I went to Canada. It was a show between two boxing clubs, St Catharines in Ontario, and Cavan Box-ing Club. St Catharines would have sent a list of boxers over to Cavan – 'This is who we have' – and the Cavan coach, Brian McKeown, would have looked at the list: 'Have – have – have – don't have, but I can sort a boxer from a different club, if she wants to come.' I was asked, and I wanted to go. It was the first time I'd boxed for another club but I've often done it since. I boxed for Antrim against a team from Spain; I fought Miriam Gutiérrez, who fought Katie Taylor as a professional years later. I've boxed for clubs all over the country.

We were in Canada for a week. Paul Barbour, a boxer from

Banbridge in County Down, went too. I remember going to this amusement park, and into a haunted castle. All the lights were off, and someone grabbed my leg. The walls were closing in, getting smaller; I literally thought my life was over. It was pitch black and I was screaming and clinging on to Paul for dear life. It was brilliant.

One of the St Catharines coaches had a barbecue at his house, and we all went there; it was great craic. The whole trip was absolutely class. I didn't want to come home. And I won my fight, against Renelle Minott. I was more experienced than she was, and better; that was how it felt.

In August I was back in Liverpool, for the European Union Championships. To be fighting for my country, going out with the nation's flag on my chest – it felt great. It's an honour. At that stage in women's boxing in Ireland, I think the attitude was, 'Let's send them over and see how they get on.' But Katie was the World champion and I was just delighted to be on the same team as her.

I was drawn against Larisa Rosu, from Romania. It was a good fight and I held my own. But I lost, fair and square. I wasn't a million miles away from winning, and it was good to have an idea of where I was at, but I was disappointed. If I'd been a bit fitter, I could probably have won: I remember thinking that. I could have shaded it. I was fit running, I was fit training. But I think I could have been fitter psychologically.

I found it hard to breathe, sometimes. I think it was nerves; your nervous energy can sap the life out of you, and I'd be really tired in the last round. When I was younger, the GP told my Ma to put me on an inhaler. She never did, and I'm glad she didn't. I didn't feel like I needed it. I think the problem was more psychological. I still get tired in the third round now, but not *as* tired, because I'm more relaxed.

*

After leaving the Army, I went back to Youthreach. I felt that it was my home. I went to the Transition Centre on Parnell Square this time, because I was eighteen. I was in the sports programme. Noel White and Ger Power were in charge, and Joan Burke was there as well. We'd go out to Ballymun, to the Dublin City Council gym – it's a really great gym. I was in the football group, although I didn't play football; I'd signed up to it because it was a sporty group. If they were doing drills or training, I'd get involved. But for matches, I'd just sit at the side. I'd tried, but I never felt comfortable playing football. In boxing, it's just me against one opponent and I'm constantly involved in the fight. If I switch off for a minute, I'm out. But any time I tried to play football, there were too many people on the pitch and I didn't have the ball for long enough; I lost interest and switched off, really quickly.

There used to be what the IABA called National Squad Training, for females, in the National Stadium. I was invited to take part, and the IABA sent the notification to Corinthians. Pete Taylor was the Head Coach for women's boxing, and Anja Norman organized the sessions. Sometimes Pete took the sessions, and sometimes it was other coaches. We'd be on the floor, twenty or thirty women ready to go, wondering who was actually going to take the session. It felt like the IABA wanted to be seen to be doing something about women's boxing but, really, they weren't doing a whole lot.

I'd been very excited going to squad training the first few times. I wanted to be a better boxer. I wanted to be given a chance, and I wanted to be looked after properly. The way you grow as an athlete is to surround yourself with great athletes. I could have learnt so much training with Michael Conlan and Paddy Barnes and Kenny Egan, and Katie Taylor. But it just wasn't happening, and that made it really hard.

My cousin Tanya was getting married on 11th September 2009, and I was going to be her bridesmaid. That was a week before we were due to fly out to the European Championships, in Ukraine. It was me, Sinéad and Katie who'd be going.

We were finishing training one evening in Bray. In the run-up to the Europeans, a lot of the squad training was done out in Bray, Pete's club. I felt at the time that this was just for Pete's convenience. Myself and Sinéad would get the DART together out to Bray and back – and we'd talk about how much we hated getting the DART.

This night, we were instructed to go back to our clubs to train for the the rest of the time before we travelled to Ukraine.

'Taper off in your clubs, stay sharp, and we'll send the flight details and the rest to you.'

'Grand,' I thought. 'Happy days.'

The day before Tanya's wedding, I got a message: Training tomorrow. I wasn't going to be able to make it, because I was my cousin's bridesmaid. I explained this, but I was told that it wasn't good enough. I'd have to turn up for training or I'd be off the team.

I was hysterical – in bits.

The following morning, the day of the wedding, the phone rang. It was Pete. I didn't answer at first, because I was afraid I'd be told that I wasn't going to the Europeans. But eventually I answered, and was told that I had to go to training.

'I can't,' I said. 'I can't *not* do bridesmaid for my cousin, like.'

He told me I'd be jeopardizing my chances of going to the Europeans if I didn't turn up for training.

There are some things in life that can't be missed, and the wedding had been arranged long before the training. I went to Tanya's wedding. It was Tanya who'd told me that my new-born brother Joel wasn't my new sister, when I was seven.

I was called to a meeting a few days after the wedding, in the National Stadium. Pete Taylor and Pat Ryan were there. They sat me down and told me that they weren't sending me to the Europeans. I was off the team.

I didn't react in front of them. I sat there and held back the tears, although I wanted to cry. I took it on the chin.

'Okay – yeah.'

Once I was outside, the tears flew down my face. I couldn't believe it. I phoned Paddy Osborne. He wasn't too happy about it. I phoned my family; they were really upset. I'd been training for it, and I'd been so excited.

I'm not aware that there was any build-up to their decision not to bring me. We'd been training out in Bray. I've been told since that it was *additional* training and that the normal training was in the National Stadium, but my recollection is that most – nearly all – of the training was in Bray, Pete's club. I remember getting the DART out, and being absolutely frozen coming out of the club after training, because we'd nowhere to change. The pub next door had agreed to let us change there, but that wasn't great; we didn't use it.

I was upset when I was told that I wasn't going, but I wasn't shocked. I was nineteen, and beginning to sense that I wasn't wanted.

I still had my boxing club. I still had my boxing family. I loved that, and I loved going down to the club, and the feeling that I'd get when I went in, and, later, when I was leaving.

'See you later, Kellie. I'll see you on Monday.'

That feeling of belonging – 'See you later, Jack,' 'See you later, Mary' – is brilliant; it means so much.

I kept at it. Other people in boxing believed in me. I just persisted. I have that staying power because of where I'm from, Dublin's inner city. I don't give a shit – I don't care what others think.

I moved out of the house on Portland Row when I was nineteen. Once I was out, me and my Ma got on great. All of a sudden, we were best friends. She even painted my new place for me.

I moved into the basement of a house on Richmond Road, near the Fairview end. Number 225. There was the kitchen and sitting room in one, a small box room, then the bedroom. I was living on my own, officially, and was on the Social Welfare rent allowance. I can't remember what the rent was but I couldn't afford it, even with the allowance. So I sublet the box room to a Polish woman, Aneta, for €100 a week. Now, I was able to pay the rent.

The first senior national championships that included women took place in the National Stadium, in February and March 2010. I was boxing at 69 kilos, which wasn't – or shouldn't have been – my weight. I'd moved up just to get a fight, because there was no one else in the 64-kilo division.

Putting on the weight takes no real ability. Losing it is the hard part. Today, 60 kilos is a natural weight for me. I have to keep an eye on it but I would never go above 4 or, maximum, 5 kilos heavier than my fight weight. But I'd moved out of my Ma's house and I'd discovered frozen batter-burgers, frozen pizzas, frozen chips, frozen everything. The Chinese takeaway was right on the corner, the chipper was right on the corner, Abrakebabra was at the top of the road. I was having a great time. I had no idea about diet.

I had two fights in the championships. First I fought Trish

Roddy from Bray Boxing Club. Trish was bigger than me, and I was struggling to breathe in the last round. She was some fighter; she didn't stop. Today, Trish reminds me of Mira Potkonen, the Finnish boxer. She kept coming at me; I'd my work cut out to beat her. Because Trish was from Bray, Pete Taylor was in her corner, and beating her – it was fuckin' great, absolutely brilliant.

A week later, I fought Jessica Lyons, from St Francis Boxing Club in Limerick, Anna Moore's club. I could hear Anna shouting for her. It was a good final, more technical than the fight against Trish. Jessica was a little bit hesitant throwing shots, and sometimes you can see punches coming when the other boxer is like that; I had more time to think. I was delighted when the fight was over and I'd beaten Jessica.

I'd won the tournament but, really, I felt that no one cared about the women. Lots of the girls who were boxing at that time just walked away. There were girls who were brilliant boxers, just as good as me, but who didn't have my resilience.

I loved the tournaments. Most of the audience were club people and family, and boxing fanatics, people who just followed the game. I'd go over to the Stadium all the time, when I wasn't boxing myself. I loved it, and I wanted to learn more. I'd be watching Michael Conlan and Paddy Barnes, seeing how good they were. Michael fought Shane Roche, who I used to spar with, and I just loved seeing them in the same ring. I was meeting people from all over Ireland and I got on with all of them. Then, when I was boxing, there'd be people from all around the country shouting for me.

Boxing in front of an audience is a performance – but I prefer to fight behind closed doors. (It was one of the reasons why boxing at the Olympics in Tokyo was great: there was no one there.) It's easier to cope when there isn't a crowd; the nerves are going and it's easier to control them.

But this is also true: when I win a fight and there are people there, it's great. Even before the fight, it can be great. I remember walking through the arena in New Delhi, at the World Championship in 2018. I was going to box against an Indian woman; the whole stadium was on wheels for this girl. I'm walking to the ring and I'm made up, I'm buzzing. I'm thinking to myself, 'I'm going to show yis now.'

I loved being the underdog.

One of the nights myself and Sinéad were training in the Bray club in 2009, before the European Championships, there were other boxers training there too, members of the club. Mandy Loughlin was one of them. Sinéad was friendly with her, but I was a bit dismissive.

'Ah – she thinks she's bleedin' deadly, that one.'

A while after that we were both boxing one night in some championship in the National Stadium, and I was after winning. I think Mandy had lost her fight. We were just chatting away. There was nothing in it; we weren't flirting or anything.

'Hard luck – are you going out tonight?'

'No.'

We exchanged numbers, just like new friends would.

'If you're ever going out, give us a shout.'

I wasn't going to message her; she wasn't going to message me.

Then, one day, I was in the gym in Finglas – another of the Dublin City Council gyms – and I met a friend of mine there.

'Here, Kellie – I met a young one you know. In the George.'

'Yeah?'

71

'Yeah – a boxer.'

'Who?'

'Mandy.'

So I texted Mandy: I believe you seen my friend Molly last night. She got back: Yeah. And we just started to message each other. And that was it – that was how we started.

6

'I'm not going to make weight,' I told him.
'I can't, like – I'm eating a fuckin' chicken
fillet roll here. There's no way, like.'
'Listen, love,' he said. 'If you don't take this fight
today, you'll never box for Ireland again.'

The World Championships were coming up in September 2010, in Barbados. The idea of going to Barbados to box was a dream. I was the national champion at 69 kilos, but I didn't want to go at that weight. I would have been floored by taller girls who were coming down in weight to make 69 kilos.

'I'll get battered out there. I'm not going in at 69 kilos.'

I was probably the heaviest I've ever been in my life, but I just wasn't a 69-kilo boxer. There was a spot at 64 kilos, so I thought I could box in Barbados at that weight.

But Alanna Audley-Murphy, who hadn't competed in the national championships, applied to box for Ireland at 64 kilos. Alanna's from Belfast, but she was living in England and was in the British Army. The IABA decided that they were going to send her.

I was like, 'You are in your fuck going to send Alanna. I'm fuckin' here – I *entered* the championships.'

So they arranged a box-off between me and Alanna, in the National Stadium. I went into it feeling really annoyed.

'Why am I even having a box-off? She doesn't even live in the bleedin' country.'

There was no boxing done; we just swung out of each other in the ring. It was like wrestling; it must have been terrible to watch. I remember seeing Katie at the side of the ring, close to Alanna's corner. Katie and Alanna were friends; they'd fought each other in the first sanctioned female fight in Ireland, in 2001, when they were teenagers. Katie was cheering for Alanna. I think that put me off a bit. I'd thought that Katie was deadly, and there she was cheering for someone else. Even though they were friends, I thought Katie could have been neutral. We were on the same team.

I think the overall score was 3–2. The judges saw Alanna landing three punches and me landing two, in four two-minute rounds – this was under the old point-scoring system. There were punches going everywhere but none of them landing. I didn't box with my head. Normally, I think my way into a fight. I try to formulate a plan and I try to stick to it. But as soon as that bell went there was no plan – it was gone. I don't think there was a straight punch thrown; everything was hooked, landing on the backs of our heads. She whispered something to me. I can't remember what it was but it pissed me off; she really got into my head. But that was my problem. She was as entitled to box for Ireland as I was, but I had a bee in my bonnet about it. And I *had* won the national championship.

Alanna beat me that night and went to Barbados, with Katie, Sinéad Kavanagh and Ceire Smith. She went, and I stayed at home.

I boxed her again, twice, and beat her both times.

I was in Youthreach one day when I got a phone call from Paddy Osborne, the secretary at Corinthians. I remember I was eating a chicken fillet roll when he called.

'Howyeh, Kellie.'

74

'What's the story, Paddy?'

'You're boxing against China later.'

'Wha'?'

'Yeah,' said Paddy. 'You have to weigh in.'

'I'm not going to make weight,' I told him. 'I can't, like – I'm eating a fuckin' chicken fillet roll here. There's no way, like.'

'Listen, love,' he said. 'If you don't take this fight today, you'll never box for Ireland again.'

I realized later – after I'd calmed down – that Paddy wasn't being literal; he was just keen for me to take the fight.

I knew who I was supposed to be fighting. Cheng Dong had won the 60-kilo silver medal at the World Championships in Barbados, the year before. Katie was the World champion; she'd beaten Cheng Dong in the final in Barbados. Cheng Dong had come to Ireland with a Chinese team, to take part in three exhibition events around the country. Katie had fought her in Dungarvan and New Ross, and had beaten her both times. But, for whatever reason, she'd decided not to fight Cheng Dong in the National Stadium.

I hung up the phone. I remember sitting in Youthreach, crying.

I rang my Da. I rang in the hope that he'd say, 'Don't mind him, love. You don't go in there unprepared. You do what's right for you.' It was what I wanted him to say. But he didn't say that; he gave me the right advice.

'Go for it,' he said. 'Go on – go over and fight her.'

I was like, 'Oh . . . Jesus Christ. All right.'

I went home and collected my stuff, and got a taxi to the Louis Fitzgerald Hotel, in Newlands Cross, for the weigh-in. I don't even know why there *was* a weigh-in – they were going to let me fight anyway. But, more importantly, I wasn't fit. I hadn't been training for an international fight, especially against the second-best 60-kilo boxer in the world.

I was bricking it.

'I'm not fit – oh my God, I'm terrified.'

Anna Moore was there. She was delighted that I'd agreed to fight, even though I hadn't really agreed; I'd been told I'd never box for Ireland again if I didn't. I've always called Anna 'the Mammy of Irish Boxing'; she's brilliant. And that day she was very encouraging.

'You can do it, Kellie.'

She gave me the whole motivational speech, but I was still dying inside. I lay on the bed in my room in the Louis, wondering what I was after getting myself into. I hadn't boxed for Ireland since 2008, nearly three years before.

'What am I even doing here? This is just crazy, the most random thing ever. I'm not ready for this, like.'

I was half-thinking of doing a runner.

At that stage, I hadn't won an international fight – except against Michelle Smith in Dungarvan, in 2006. I'd never won a fight at this level. Today, I know what proper training is. And I know that in 2011, we didn't get the training or the attention that the men were getting.

It's a very long day when you're hanging around, waiting to fight. You don't want to waste energy. Now I can handle it but back then I couldn't. I lay in the room, thinking. I was just filling a card, because Katie didn't want to box; that was what I thought.

The threat that I'd never box again for Ireland was bullshit: I know that now, but I don't think I did back then. Paddy hadn't said it with any malice; he'd just wanted to get me there to fight and he knew it would work.

I got in and I boxed Cheng Dong. It was close; I think I only lost by three points. She was a typical Chinese-style fighter – I know now. She was leggy and armey, feinting, pretending to throw, long ranged; she wouldn't get in to work close. She'd be tipping me – tip, and move, tip, and move – stepping to the side all the time. I was able to match that, because that was kind of how I boxed at the time. What I couldn't match was her fitness.

Everyone seemed a bit shocked that I did so well. But I think it was fear that got me through it more than anything else.

Anna was delighted. 'Look how close you are to the Number Two in the world!'

And I was delighted. But I still didn't really believe in myself. It's hard to be confident when you don't have proper preparation behind you. Any athlete needs to know that she's put in the right work and preparation. And she needs to know that her coaches have confidence in her. I never felt that, with the Irish women's team coaches. I felt that confidence from my club coaches but not from the Irish team coaches. The vibe wasn't right.

Anna has often reminded me about that fight against Cheng Dong.

'Remember you back then?'

We've come a long way.

After Youthreach, I enrolled at Coláiste Íde, in Finglas, as an early school leaver and did Sports and Leisure Management. Being in Coláiste Íde, I got a Social Welfare allowance, paid into my bank account. I was there for two years. I became a fitness instructor and personal trainer. I was doing something I liked, and one of the years I won Student of the Year. I couldn't believe it. I'd hated secondary school; basically, I got kicked out. But here I was, student of the year.

A few months after the Olympics, I met a child – a girl – outside my Ma's door. There was a gang of kids, and they were all around me. And the girl asked me, 'What age were you when you got into boxing? You didn't like school, didn't you not?'

'I didn't like school *then*,' I told her. 'But I think it's great now.'

The girl said, 'I tell my Ma that Kellie Harrington didn't go to school and look at *her*.'

There were lectures, but there was also a lot of physical activity, hands-on stuff – exercise to music, aerobics classes, learning how to teach it, learning about the anatomy of the body; how to instruct in a gym, the correct techniques. I knew the purpose of the course; I knew it would be two years, and that I'd have a job at the end of it. It was all about learning how to stand up and give a class. Like, cueing in: if I was giving an exercise to music, I had to learn how to time it – 'Four, three . . .' I'm on the beat, 'two, one' – and off we go. I absolutely loved it, and always got good energy from it. I liked the teachers, Claire Teague and her husband, Danny. John Farrell did first aid with us, and lifeguarding. He was very witty and sardonic. They were friendly people, smiling all the time, and they'd a great way of explaining things.

I was driving at this stage and I had my own car, an '02 Polo – it was blue. I was working part-time, and got a loan from the North Strand Credit Union; I've always been very good with managing money.

My Nanny lived just up the road from the college, and I could drive to her house for my lunch. She always had Brennans batch bread and corned beef and real butter, and oxtail soup. I spent a lot of time with her and sometimes stayed there. I'd do a lot of housework, because she was older. I was living in two places, the flat on the Richmond Road and my Nanny's.

I offered to drive her to the post office, to collect her

pension. My Grandda had passed away, so she had no one else to take her.

'D'you want me to bring you to get your pension, Nanny? Will I bring you tomorrow – d'you want me to bring you anywhere?'

But she wouldn't get into the car with me. She always got a taxi.

I moved to the WFTRA Boxing Club in Finglas because I was in Coláiste Íde and I was staying with my Nanny more often. I'd been in Corinthians a good while – years – and it was my first club, but I didn't find it hard to go. I left on good terms.

I love the WFTRA. I was there about two years. But the facilities weren't great. They used a community hall and they had to set up the ring, and take it down, every evening. It ate into the time. There were only a couple of bags, up on the stage. There was only one shower.

There were loads of women and girls training, but none participating in contests; I was the only competitive female boxer. I didn't feel anything in particular about this. When I was in the Army, I hadn't enjoyed feeling like the only woman. But in boxing I didn't feel that way. I'd just get in with the lads and I'd try to knock ten bells out of them.

Paddy Fitzpatrick was the coach at the WFTRA, and Leo Keogh was there too. Leo lived about four houses up from my Nanny's. He had millions of grandchildren and they were training in the club too. It was like other boxing clubs; you became part of the family. I'd drop in to Leo's house and have a cup of tea. He had birds in a shed in the back of his garden. There was a huge cage full of finches. He bred them – zebra finches, goldfinches. They were beautiful, all different colours. He played music to them, on a CD player. He was just such a lovely man, like a second granddad.

I left WFTRA around the time I finished at Coláiste Íde, and went back to Corinthians. It wasn't a big, dramatic decision. I wasn't going out to Finglas as often now, and I was living on Richmond Road, not far from Corinthians. Every time there was a club show – a tournament – I'd get tickets and invite Leo and Paddy, even though they weren't my coaches any more. They always came along, whenever I was boxing in Ireland.

Years later, Leo got cancer and became very sick, very quickly. He was a big, big man: we used to call his hands shovels. The story was, his hands were that big because when he was younger there were so many of them in the family that he used to reach in and grab all the food with one hand.

I went to see Leo in hospital, in the Intensive Care Unit. I brought the gold medal I'd won in the World Championships in 2018. My Da came with me. Two of Leo's granddaughters, Amy and Emma, were there, outside the ICU.

'Kellie, he's probably not going to recognize you – he's really not great.'

'Don't worry about it. I just want to go in and pay my respects.'

So I went in.

Leo was a very proud man. He didn't want anyone to see him the way he was. He was just a frame of himself. He tried to sit up in bed and the tears came down his face.

'I always knew you'd do it,' he said.

He took my hand.

'You did it for Finglas.'

I was trying not to cry. I was trying to be as upbeat as I

could. I looked across at my Da. He was standing in the corner, also trying not to cry.

'There you go, Leo,' I said. 'I told you I'd do it, didn't I? When I was over there I said I was going to do it for you, and I was going to bring the medal back and show you.'

'I'm so proud of you,' he said. 'I always knew you'd do it. And you're going to do it again.'

7

She beat me fair and square; she was the better boxer.
But again, there was tension in the Ireland set-up –
something wasn't right. I just knew
I wasn't wanted there.

Pete Taylor told me that I would beat anybody in Europe at 69 kilos, that no one would get near me. But I knew: at that weight, I was small and fat. I made weight at 64 kilos very easily and I'd only fought at 69 kilos once before – because there was no one available to box at 64 kilos. I couldn't beat most of my opponents at 64 kilos. I wasn't going to win at 69 kilos. At that weight, I would have been 9 kilos heavier than Katie. I think he was keeping me away from her.

I worshipped the ground that Katie Taylor walked on. I thought she was brilliant. And I'd never, ever thought of fighting her because, at that time, I was afraid of her.

Just before my first fight in the European Union Championships, in Katowice, Poland, in 2011, Pete spoke to me. I was about to go into the ring against Oliwia Łuczak, a Polish woman, at 64 kilos. And Pete was telling me, 'She's a good girl, this one. Katie beat her, but she's good – but Katie *did* beat her. You should be okay with her.'

It was very offputting, coming just before I was getting in to fight. I'd hardly spoken to Pete during that trip, except when I was getting warmed up before the fight. I was thinking, 'Oh,

Jesus, Katie fought her – Katie's brilliant, so this girl is at Katie's level.' He was my coach on that trip but, really, he wasn't coaching me. No other coach had ever said anything like that to me before a fight, literally five minutes before walking to the ring. I don't think I ever had a proper coaching conversation with Pete on any boxing trip. His focus was always on Katie and not the other women boxers. And I don't think Katie ever did fight Łuczak – maybe in an exhibition, but not a carded, competitive fight.

I lost. Łuczak beat me fair and square; she was the better boxer. But again, there was tension in the Ireland set-up – something wasn't right. I just knew I wasn't wanted there.

The general attitude of the IABA towards women's boxing really annoyed me. Women weren't being looked after; just one woman – Katie – was. And the IABA were letting this happen. The women weren't getting the opportunity to train with the best, and they weren't being sent to the multinations training camps and tournaments that the men were being sent to.

I put up a post on Facebook, giving out about Katie and her Da, the preferential treatment that Katie was getting, and how the rest of the women weren't getting treated equally. I was lashing the IABA out of it; I called them a bunch of biscuit-eating bastards – which wasn't very clever of me. Pete sent in a letter of complaint, and I was brought up in front of the disciplinary board.

I was worried that I wouldn't be sent to the European Championships – a bigger deal than the European Union Championships. I'd have stood my ground if it hadn't been for the Europeans. I'd already missed out on the Worlds in Barbados, and I'd been dropped from the last Europeans because I'd gone to my cousin's wedding. I didn't want to be dropped again. I had to come up with some excuse, and fast. So I decided to blame it on my cousin Michael.

I asked him.

'Grand – yeah, no bother. They *are* a bunch of biscuit-eating bastards. You're right.'

I did a back-pedaller; I denied the whole thing,

'It wasn't me – it was my cousin. He was going mad 'cause he knows everything that's going on and he's not happy with it. He wrote that on my page, but I didn't know. As soon as I saw it, I deleted it.'

Pete Taylor didn't turn up for the hearing, so the complaint was dismissed. The board advised me to make sure that in future I was the only one who had access to my Facebook account. I must have done a good job of convincing them that I hadn't written the post. Anna Moore was on the board, and even she believed me. But she didn't think that what I'd posted was a big deal, and said so. Anna always had my back.

I shouldn't have put it out there in the first place, for everyone to see and comment on; I wasn't very strategic in my approach. I was hotheaded back then; I didn't know how to handle my feelings. Today, I can manage my honesty and emotions a lot better.

A few months later, at the European Championships in Rotterdam, I was having problems with my feet. They get very sore, awful pain at the outer sides, from my baby toes down to my heels, and I can't move them properly. Besides having flat feet I have a condition called *plantar fasciitis*. The pain can be excruciating. It's as if they're cramping up; it's horrible. The more I move, the more it hurts – and moving is one of my strengths as a boxer. The pain becomes the preoccupation; it's all I can think of. I don't think twice when I'm punched in the face, because of the adrenaline. I'm thinking about how to respond to it, and how to win the point back. But when my feet start to hurt, I feel it straight away. Before a fight, it's a huge distraction.

In Rotterdam, the pain was really bad.

I told Pete, 'I'm wearing runners.'

He said that if I wore runners the judges would give the fight against me, because they'd think I was a novice. But I fought in the runners, regardless. I felt better in them; my feet weren't as sore. I boxed Martina Schmoranzova from the Czech Republic. It was a very close fight. It was very tactical; she was a tricky southpaw, and she'd come down from 69 kilos. She was very smart. She wasn't world class but, because of my lack of experience and preparation, she seemed world class. She was fitter than me. That was what it came down to – fitness and confidence, and experience. A little bit more of these things, and the fight would have been different. But she beat me.

Pete was saying, 'I told you you shouldn't have worn the runners.'

It wasn't what I needed to hear. This was just after the fight. The woman had beaten me; it had nothing to do with the runners. It was the last time Pete Taylor was in my corner. I don't remember it being a decision; it just happened that way.

I still think, today, that he did what he had to do to make Katie a success. An athlete often has to be ruthless, and so does the coach. Unfortunately, I got a taste of that ruthlessness, and so did some of the others. Pete wouldn't let anyone get in the way, or distract him from the rhythm of his work with Katie.

I'd lost my fight, and Sinéad Kavanagh had lost hers, that same day. I was in my room, and Sinéad was in hers. A team meeting had been called – there were regular team meetings – and myself and Sinéad both independently decided that we wouldn't go. I was still very upset. But I was told – again – that I'd never box for Ireland again if I didn't go. So I told Anna, the team manager, that I had a dose of the runs. I didn't want to sit there and talk about my fight. It was still very fresh; I just needed time.

I don't think Sinéad bothered making an excuse.

I stayed in my room, reliving the fight and wondering about what I was doing. Nothing was going right. My head was fried. Why was I losing all of my international fights? And why wouldn't I be boxing for Ireland again just because I hadn't gone to a bloody meeting?

I heard no more about it. The next day I was back out, supporting the other women in the team who were left in the tournament. It was the thing I really enjoyed, the friendship with my teammates. But the words – the threat that I wouldn't box for Ireland again – hung there. It was a bad time. I was twenty-one; I didn't have the experience to deal with it, to see it for what it was, an idle threat. But after a few days I was grand again.

Me and Mandy were over at the National Stadium one night, watching the boxing, and we didn't get back to Richmond Road until about a quarter to twelve.

I hadn't really seen myself in a relationship with a woman until I met Mandy. And that came at the right time. I was twenty when we met; I was very immature. Mandy brought stability to my life. She was very independent. It's the old saying, 'Iron sharpens iron.' I matured a lot when I met her.

We were together about six months when I told my parents – but they already knew.

'What d'you think we are, like – d'you think we're stupid

or wha'? Of course yis're together. You're attached at the hip.'

I had a pit bull terrier, Roxy, and a Staffordshire bull terrier, Macy. I kept them in the garden, at the front of the house, when I wasn't there. It was walled, so they couldn't get out.

To get into my flat, we went down some steps at the back of the house; the door was to the left, straight into the bedroom. There was a bathroom, then the little hallway and the box room, where Aneta was staying; then there was the sitting room/kitchen – one room. There was another door that led out to where the dogs were.

I'd jumped into the shower, but I heard Mandy.

'Kellie, there's people outside spitting at the dogs.'

We always left a big pot of water outside for the dogs. So I shouted from the shower:

'If they don't fuck off, tell them you're going to drown them with the water.'

I didn't think she'd actually do something like that.

There were two of them, drunk, a man and a woman. They were leaning over, putting their hands through the railings, spitting, and trying to clatter the dogs. Mandy was shouting at them to go away. The man was about six foot and the woman was four foot nothing. Normally, you'd be afraid to put your hand near a pit bull, but my lads would have licked you to death.

The drunk couple wouldn't go away; the dogs weren't frightening them. So Mandy threw the water over them.

I was out of the shower, drying off, and they were still outside, still trying to clatter the dogs. The drenching hadn't worked.

I walked out.

'Listen – just fuck off. Get away!'

The woman came at me, trying to kick me and belt me. I kept pushing her off, but she was swinging at me. She was off her face, and shouting weird, vulgar stuff at us.

I said to Mandy, 'Right – they're going to keep coming at us. You'll have to take her and I'll have to take him.'

Her face dropped. Mandy had never hit anyone outside of a boxing ring in her life.

'Mandy – I'm going to have to hit her.'

The woman ran at me again and I sidestepped her and, as I did, I hit her. She fell straight into the garden. Then the fella was squaring up to me. He would have flattened me.

I was going, 'Come on – come on – !'

I was backing off, trying to get away from the house.

In the meantime, Mandy had phoned my Ma and Da. My Da was on his way down on his pushbike and my Ma and my brother Joel were in a taxi.

The Garda came along and they moved the man and the woman on. Then the two of them turned, and started coming back down towards us again. The Garda got out of the car and your one – the woman – gave him a boot in the leg, then ran off up the road.

Another time, we were in the kitchen, having our dinner, the tea and biscuits after, when I heard the door from outside into the bedroom banging a bit, like it was caught in a draught. I went out to see what was causing the banging.

My knicker drawer had been emptied onto the bed. It didn't really register at first that there was someone in the room. But then I saw a foot behind the door.

'Ha ha ha – very fuckin' funny.'

I thought it was one of my mates, getting ready to jump out. But a handbag went into the air and a fella I'd never seen before started running – out, and up the steps.

I got an almighty fright, and I ran after him. I grabbed him from behind and, as I did that, I gave him a dig and he dropped to the ground. I pulled him away from the door, onto the street, so there'd be people there to see what was happening and, with a bit of luck, help me.

'It wasn't me, love! It wasn't me – I was doing the shop for yeh!'

I had my knee on his chest and I was battering him. A big German fella from the house next door came out, holding a pole.

'That is *gut*, Kellie – that is *gut*.'

The size of him – I thought he might intervene, that he'd help me hold the fella down. But he stayed where he was, encouraging me.

'That is *gut*.'

Mandy had come out. Her biscuits and tea had been disturbed, so she looked up and down the street, then kicked your man and went back into the house. I think it was the first time she ever hit someone, outside of the ring. I was proud of her!

I was there, holding your man down, and a car pulled in. The guy in the car thought I was just randomly battering some fella. But he figured out what was happening and he put your man under citizen's arrest! And the Guards came along, from Clontarf Station.

'What's going on here?'

Your man who'd put the robber under citizen's arrest obviously thought he was the dog's bollix. He took over – he was going on about what he'd done. I was wondering, 'Who *is* he?' And your man, the robber, was sitting on the wall.

'It wasn't bleedin' me – ! I was only going to the shops for her.'

There was blood all over his face. The Guards knew who he was. They were putting him into the back of the car.

'You bleedin' rat,' he said to me.

They took him away. But I was confused – it was all a bit mad – and I was getting anxious: 'I'm after giving him an awful beating – he's going to come back later.'

I rang the Guards at Clontarf Station.

'Look – I'm terrified. What's going to happen now?'

'Listen, love – he's going to be in custody for the weekend. He'll be going into court on Monday.'

'Where does he live?'

'We can't tell you that, but he's staying about ten minutes away from you.'

It turned out that he was from the Diamond, near where I'm from, and he was a cousin of my Ma's old next-door neighbour.

The Guards came back later to take a statement from me.

'So, Kellie – how did you hold this man down?'

'Well, when I came out, I saw him with the bag, so I grabbed him, gave him a dig, pulled him out to the road, hit him—'

The Guard looked at me.

'So – you came out, he fell over and you held him.'

'No, no – when I came out, I grabbed him, I gave him a dig, he fell, and—'

'So, he fell over –'

I copped on.

'Yeah. He fell over and I just held him till yis came.'

The tournament was called the Haringey Box Cup, and it was run by the Haringey Boxing Club, in London. It was my idea to go. I'd heard about it from other boxers, and I wanted the experience. I wanted to get fights outside of Ireland. We'd paid for it out of our own pockets, and I got sponsorship to help me pay my way.

Mandy was with me, and my friend Dervla Duffy; Dervla was boxing for Ryston Boxing Club in Kildare. The Alexandra Palace, the Ally Pally, where it was taking place, was massive. They had six rings set up. It's one of the biggest box cups in Europe, and I was really excited to be there. I was fighting at 60 kilos, because I wasn't representing Ireland; I was boxing for Corinthians. Katie, quite rightly, was Ireland's 60-kilo boxer, but I could fight at 60 in the box cups.

It was a three-day tournament and I fought on all three, because I got to the final. My opponent in the final was Fam Elgan from Norway. I remember watching one of her earlier fights.

'Oh my God – she is an animal.'

She was smaller than me, and well built. Back then, in 2012, I would have looked at my opponents on YouTube and I'd have thought, 'Oh my God, look at how good she is.' It never occurred to me how bad her opponent might have been. When I looked up Fam Elgan on YouTube I discovered that she was a World-champion kick-boxer.

'Ah – she's bleedin' deadly.'

I was sitting near the ring, waiting for the final, when Fam came over and sat right in front of me. She put her earphones in and stared at me, trying to intimidate me. I just sat there. She was pretty but she had an aggressive, mean expression on her face.

'Oh, for fuck sake – this is going to be hard work.'

She was a very explosive boxer, and powerful. But the same punch worked on her, over and over and over again. All I could hear was people going, 'Sidestep, sidestep, sidestep!' She kept coming forward and I just kept sidestepping her. And after I sidestepped, I stepped in again with a right hand, and back out.

I could hear Mandy and Dervla.

'Ah, lovely – !'

'Ah – beautiful!'

I won the fight, and I was delighted, because she was class, a very technical fighter. And it was brilliant, winning a tournament outside Ireland. That was *my* Olympics.

I watched Katie in the final of the 2012 Olympics in London. I watched all of her fights. And I was made up for her when she won. It was amazing. But I never thought, 'I'm going to do what's she's done.' I'd been to the Europeans, but I hadn't won a fight.

I wasn't aware yet about the need to look after my diet; I hadn't a clue. Mandy was living with me some of the time, and she went down the slippery slope of eating shite – tubs of ice cream every night, and takeaways. Eventually, she decided that enough was enough. She was still boxing. She'd left Bray and joined Corinthians too. When she got stricter about what she ate, so did I. Mandy changed the way I ate, and what I ate. I went from frozen food to fresh food. Instead of eating batter-burgers, we were eating burgers without the batter!

Jimmy Halpin was one of my coaches at Corinthians. He was one of the best coaches in Ireland, and one of the first to make me begin to believe in myself. He was very technical, and he helped me work on the technical side of my boxing. He had coached Darren Sutherland, who'd won a bronze medal in Beijing in 2008, and other good boxers who I knew and had seen fight. Jimmy was able to put training plans together that helped me to back up physically what I wanted to do technically. He saw how good I was, and I started to accept what he was saying to me.

I'd started inviting boxers – girls – over from different countries, for training camps, to spar with me. I had plenty of possible sparring partners in Ireland, but they were men. There were very few women of a high enough quality; and if I sparred with the same women over and over, or the same lads, we'd become too familiar with one another; it would be the same spar every time. Katie didn't spar with females; Pete didn't want her sparring with them. I asked for it, but it never happened. I was happy sparring with men, but men – because they're stronger – will hold back with some power when they're sparring with a woman. I'd still be getting a good spar, but I felt that I needed to measure myself with women in my weight category. I needed – for example – to know how a woman was going to hit, so I wouldn't be shocked if she hit hard; she wouldn't be holding anything back fighting another woman. And if I was going to get better, I had to challenge myself. Someone from outside, someone I didn't know, would be pushing me. And they'd be turning up to try and get the better of me.

I invited Fam Elgan to Ireland, after I'd fought her at the Ally Pally. I knew how good she was. Internationally, she wasn't well known, but sometimes there are great boxers out there and their countries don't really give them a chance. I was beginning to recognize a challenge when I saw it, and I knew that Fam was a challenge to me. I'd fought Fam, and I thought she was fantastic; I loved the way she moved in the ring. Not just sparring – I wanted to train alongside someone like her. So I invited her over, put her up in my house, and we had a week's training and sparring camp. It was a really great, tough week. I wanted to see what she did, and how hard she trained, what she was like on the bags. I was watching what she was doing and learning from her.

I'm classed as a universal boxer, which means I can fight both orthodox and southpaw; I change all the time. I can't write with my left hand, but I can box with it. Everything I can do on my right side as a boxer, I can do on my left.

When I first started to box, in Corinthians, that was the way I boxed; it was just what I did. Everything I did on one side, I'd do on the other side. If I learnt how to throw a left-left-right, I'd then switch and I'd throw a right-right-left. It's a massive asset.

It's what won me the Olympics. I lost the first round in the final, and when I came back out I changed, totally, into the opposite stance. I won the second round, and then the third. I went from orthodox to southpaw, and I kept changing – orthodox, southpaw, orthodox, southpaw – throughout the fight. It's very off-putting for the opponent.

For an orthodox boxer fighting a southpaw, it's a battle to keep her left foot on the outside of the southpaw's right foot. But when I'm fighting a southpaw, I keep changing my stance, and I do it so quickly she doesn't realize I've changed. Sometimes I don't realize it myself, it comes that naturally. She throws something stupid, as if I'm still in the orthodox stance. But now I'm in the opposite stance and she hasn't registered it yet, so she's exposed and I counter with whatever I want to counter with.

Some people told me to stop doing it, probably because at first I was crap at it. But Joey didn't discourage me; he did pads with me from both sides. Joey had learnt a lot from a Cuban coach, Nicolás Cruz Hernandez, who took Michael Carruth to the 1992 Olympics, where Michael won the gold medal. Nicolás Cruz Hernandez coached in Corinthians for a while, when Joey was younger. Joey took a lot of what he learnt from Cruz Hernandez. And that Cuban style, which is very universal, became my style of boxing.

I started to watch Michael Conlan fight in the National Stadium when he was only a youth. He was a couple of years younger than me, and he changed stance all the time. He could fight long range, middle range, close range – all the different variations. He wasn't a one-trick pony.

'Michael Conlan's boxing tonight – Jesus, I can't wait for that.'

He just got better and better. He qualified for the Olympic Games in 2012, and went there and got a bronze; he was only twenty years old, a nipper. So I was watching him all along. I loved the way he carried himself, as a person. I thought to myself, 'He's class – he's a good role model.'

I was looking at fights and examining the strategies. If I'm in at short range and my opponent is right in front of me, I can't throw a straight punch. Everything I throw is going to be short, bent-arm punching. With mid range, I have to make sure that I'm always moving. I'm waiting, and I've got to be able to slip, so I can throw a straight punch back. Then with long-distance punches – I'm not going to land a punch from too far out, so I have to do something, walk in, or jump in, to cover the space and get the punch in.

If I meet another tactical boxer who moves a lot, I have to cut her off. There's no point just chasing her. She's moving to her left, or to her right, so I need to be able to step my foot across and cut her off, stop her from moving that way. As soon as she starts to go the other way, I can jump in with a shot.

I was having to learn all of this, but it wasn't just useful; I loved it.

8

I loved the job, but it could be a bit upsetting.
Some of the patients had nothing – no family coming
in to see them; it was heartbreaking. They were lovely
people who'd been dealt a shit hand.

I'd started working in St Vincent's Psychiatric Hospital, in
Fairview, while I was still at Coláiste Íde. I was living nearby,
on the Richmond Road, and I left in my CV. I applied for a
catering/cleaning job – a domestic. I got a letter back: they
were very sorry but they weren't looking for staff at that time.
But a few months later I got another letter: now they were
looking for staff and they asked me to come up for an inter-
view. So I went up and I got the job – my first proper job.

I'd worked in Burger King in Finglas for about a week. My
cousin Hazel was the manager in a different Burger King,
and she got me in. I started with another girl, but neither of
us had a clue. I'd be on the till and she'd be back doing the
food. Someone ordered a veggie burger and she sent me out
a bun with lettuce and tomato but no actual burger. I'd no
idea what a veggie burger was.

The customer came back.

'I asked for a bleedin' veggie burger – what the fuck is
this?'

'It's a burger with veg in it, like.'

'It's only a bit of lettuce and a slice of fuckin' tomato.'

Me and the other girl would take our breaks together and

we'd sit down and have Whopper Meals and ice creams, and apple tarts. We lasted a week before we were politely let go.

Immediately after finishing in Coláiste Íde, I got a job at a gym in Sandymount, while continuing to work part-time at Vincent's. I felt that it was something I needed to do: I'd done the two years in college to become a fitness instructor. But I quickly realized that it wasn't what I'd been hoping for. I stuck at it for two years but I thought that the staff, including me, were under-appreciated, undervalued – and the wages were absolutely shit. I was getting a tenner an hour. I was constantly having to learn off choreographed routines, and me and choreography have never been the best of friends. I hated it. I'd be at home, looking at DVDs of the exercises I'd have to do the next day – all for a tenner an hour. I was working in Westwood and in the hospital, *and* I was training. So I said, 'I'll knock that gym on the head.'

I kept being asked why I didn't leave the hospital instead. But the hospital was great. It's no one's idea of a glamorous lifestyle, but I loved it. I felt that what I did was of value, and I felt valued too. I was only cleaning, but someone had to do that job. It's vital work. It's not that I love cleaning; I'm not a massive fan of it. But what I really liked was the contact with the patients.

It was a new scene for me, and an eye-opener. I was seeing people who were mentally unwell, seeing people in ways that we don't usually see them. I loved the job, but it could be a bit upsetting. Some of the patients had nothing – no family coming in to see them; it was heartbreaking. They were lovely people who'd been dealt a shit hand.

It was difficult not to take it with me when I was going home – I was often saddened – but in many ways it was great. I always tried to make people laugh, even at my own expense;

I'd make an eejit out of myself to give them a laugh, and that made me feel good.

I remember there was one patient whose room I had to clean.

'You'd better not go near my bleedin' floor with that smelly disinfectant.'

'I'm not going near your room,' I'd tell her. 'If you don't want me to do it, don't worry. D'you think I'd do something like that without asking you?'

'Nah – fuckin' smelly mop and smelly disinfectant.'

'Don't worry – I'm not touching it.'

As soon as she went downstairs I'd be in and I'd be mopping the room as quick as I could. My heart would be pounding; I'd be sweating with the fear that she was going to come back and catch me in her room with the smelly mop.

I'd be back out and on the landing when she was coming back up.

'I hope you didn't bleedin' go in while I was gone.'

'I wasn't anywhere near your room.'

She'd go into her room.

'You were in here?!'

'I wasn't in – no. That's the smell from outside, like. You're smelling the room next door.'

These things happened all the time.

The building was huge and old, and there was a spookiness, an eerie atmosphere. It reminded me of Gormanston Barracks. If I was cleaning the toilets and I heard a noise, I'd be jumping.

'Is someone there? Is someone there?'

But I loved it. It was such a new experience. There was a nurse there when I started, Dermot Colgan; I never met anyone who was as good with people as Dermot. He was like everybody's da – he was like *my* Da. Watching him work, the way he interacted with the patients – it was sometimes hard to differentiate between him and the people he was with; it was just magic. He could talk them down if they they got out of hand; he'd a way of changing the way they were thinking. He'd cook the patients a fry at the weekends; they'd get sausages and rashers, and French toast. He made the hospital like a home. All the patients loved it when he was on. I'd hear it all day – 'Dermot?', 'Dermot?', 'Dermot?' Everyone wanted him for something; they wanted to be with him. The nurses' shifts were really long. By the third day of the four-day shift, a nurse's demeanour would often change; they wouldn't have the same spark. But Dermot was always the same, always relaxed.

The ward I worked in when I started has since closed, and most of the patients went out into different community settings. The last patient left in the ward had got to know me, and he'd often give me a hug; he was the last man in this huge building.

Dermot was on duty one day. I told him I wanted to bring my dog Macy in, to meet this patient.

He thought about it for a second.

'All right.'

This wasn't allowed. Macy wasn't a therapy dog; she was a Staffordshire bull terrier. But I knew my dog and I knew she'd be great. So I brought her in and I let her off the lead. She was running around, and she went up to the patient. He was delighted. He sat down and the dog jumped up on the chair beside him, then onto his lap; she was licking his face.

'Relax,' I told Macy. 'Stop licking him.'

But the man's face – he looked so happy. It was a special little moment. He was buzzing after it. And so was I.

*

The Golden Girl Box Cup takes place every year in Borås, in southern Sweden. I went there in early 2013 with Mandy, who boxed in the tournament as well. It was really exciting, because there were loads of other Irish boxers going too – all of them girls, all different ages.

I loved the atmosphere of the box cups, which had nothing to do with the Ireland set-up, and seeing all these new female boxers. There was a real sense of excitement.

'Is she any good? What weight is she? Who has she boxed? What is she like?'

Ida Lundblad, my first opponent, was supposed to be the next big thing in Sweden. I'd heard about her before I even got to Sweden, and I was visualizing Superwoman.

'I'm boxing a Swede in Sweden – I won't be getting the decision here.'

It was January, and it was freezing. I remember walking from our hotel to the weigh-in, through falling snow. It was a fresh cold feeling; it wasn't damp. I had a big Converse bomber jacket, and I was quite warm in it; and I had a lovely pair of thick cotton tracksuit bottoms. I remember, we were sitting at a window in a restaurant, looking out at the snow. I was thinking about my fight later that day.

'Wouldn't it be great if I didn't actually *have* to fight later on?'

It was a competitive fight, but I won it. I was very pleasantly surprised, particularly because I was boxing at 60 kilos. At that time, around 2012 and 2013, I was fluctuating between 60 and 64 kilos. I couldn't box for Ireland at 60 kilos because Katie boxed at 60. At international level, only one boxer can be sent at each weight. Katie was Ireland's boxer at 60 kilos, and rightly so. She was the European champion, she was the World champion, she was the Olympic champion. It wasn't a case of me or her; she deserved it. I think that if more time and effort, and thought, had been put into me, I would have done well at 64 kilos. I wasn't getting beaten because of my weight; I was being beaten because I wasn't being prepared properly. But I was never really a 64-kilo boxer – this was something I was beginning to understand – and whenever I got a chance, I'd go at 60 kilos.

I'd been boxing a Swede in her own country, so I felt I must have deserved the result. I was delighted.

I boxed Anastasia Gorazhdantseva from Russia the next day, and I won again. It was great fighting so soon after the first fight. I love boxing but I also like to get it over with; I don't like the waiting.

My fight with Gorazhdantseva was quite late at night. Normally, if you fight at night, your next fight won't be until late enough the following day. It gives you time to rest. And that was the plan this time; I'd be boxing Mira Potkonen from Finland the next afternoon. I went down that morning for my weigh-in. I was sitting there, waiting, and I got a phone call from the organizers. They told me the Finland team were hoping to move the fight, so they could catch an earlier train home. I said no; I was wrecked and needed the time for recovery. But they kept at it and basically guilted me into agreeing to box at the earlier time.

I'd seen Mira Potkonen warming up. She looked tall – taller than me – from the other side of the warm-up area. But when we got into the ring, she wasn't particularly tall. The fight started, and I remember thinking, 'Jesus Christ – this one is very awkward.' She was unreadable. She could hit me from anywhere, at any time. Still, I thought I fought better than her. My work was cleaner, and I looked the better boxer. I was the one who was landing the cleaner punches, not throwing them into the air. I thought I'd shaded it. But she beat me by two points.

I went up to the organizers.

'I actually did a good thing coming down here today. I should have been allowed proper recovery but I obliged you. There was no fairness in that result.'

I never went back to that tournament. Now, I know it's more about the experience than it is about the result. Really, I was biting my nose to spite my face.

I'd be meeting Mira Potkonen again.

There was an international training camp before we went to the 2013 European Union Championships – I think it was in the High Performance Unit gym at the National Stadium. The Irish girls and a team from Germany were training together. Gerry Storey and Paddy Hughes, from Ryston Boxing Club in Kildare, were running the camp. Dervla Duffy was there too, and Ceire Smith, Michaela Walsh, Christina Desmond, Aoife Burke and Sinéad Kavanagh. Katie was training separately, with the men's team. Gerry Storey had taken over as women's head coach by then. Pete was coaching Katie.

We'd been training for a week, and at the end of it there were going to be test matches, as a reward for the work done. There were more Irish women than Germans, so not all the Irish girls would get a match. I was one of the boxers selected.

But then they tried to do me out of the test match. I don't really know who made the decision but the coaches told me that they wanted to put Katie in instead of me.

I flipped the lid; I really lost the head.

'Wha'? What?!'

And I was called up to another discipinary meeting. This time I had it out with them.

'I've been here all week. I've been fuckin' training here all week and there's no way I'm not getting a fight on the show.

I'm the one who's been here, with the team. I turned up every day, and you're trying to take that away from me.'

I don't think they really knew what to do. So, instead of taking the fight from me, they took it from some other girl. The Association's attitude to women's boxing was terrible. They didn't see past Katie. And if she hadn't achieved what she did, they wouldn't have thought about women's boxing at all.

The European Union Championships were in Hungary, in Keszthely. I wasn't feeling great about going. There wasn't much of the excitement I'd felt going to Haringey and Borås. I was going to be boxing at 64 kilos, and I wasn't really a 64-kilo boxer. I knew that now.

I was sharing a room with Aoife Burke and Christina Desmond. The room was tiny. We were nearly spooning, the three beds were so close. And it was roasting. When we opened the window, flies took over the room.

The food was terrible. I couldn't eat it. Other people on the team were eating in restaurants, but I'd brought very little money with me; I hadn't been expecting to buy my own food. I was paying rent at home, and I had a credit union loan. I just didn't have much money and what little I had I spent on food. I'd brought some snacks with me, but I'd eaten them. I'd no money left and I was too proud to ask the team managers for any so I could get something decent to eat.

Between the heat and not eating enough, I weighed in at sixty-one point something. I had a bowl of muesli and a Snickers bar before the fight. I was boxing Bianka Nagy, a Hungarian. She'd come down from 69 kilos. She was massive.

My Irish friends and the German girls from the training camp in Dublin were around the ring, cheering for me. During the first two rounds, I could hear them going, 'Yeah – oh, yes!' and clapping me.

Then it changed.

'Oooh – !'

'Aww – !'

I was getting battered from pillar to post. I had nothing; I was gone. There was the heat, and I'd nothing inside me; I hadn't eaten properly. I looked at Nagy's corner. They were making hand signals, urging her to push forward, to finish me off. I was being hammered, and I was trying to hold on.

I got back to the corner after the third round and Gerry Storey, the coach, was there. Gerry Storey is a lovely man. He's a big part of Irish boxing history; he has coached so many great boxers.

'You're doing great, love – jab, jab.'

I remember thinking, 'Jab, jab? I'm getting the bleedin' head pummelled off me. Jab, jab is not working!'

She won, on a split decision. It could have gone either way, but she got it. She deserved it. I'd given her a boxing lesson for the first two rounds, but then – *bump* – I shut down. I was done; I'd nothing left.

After the fight, I had to be helped out of the ring. I had to put my arms around Gerry and another man's shoulders. They had to lay me out on the floor, and throw water over me. I was over-heated. I was starving. I couldn't wait to get out of there. I had a proper black eye, the first I'd ever had; it was swollen out and everything.

I knew why I'd lost. There was the heat, but it was really about not having food – and not being looked after.

I always say to coaches, 'Make sure you ask the boxers if they've pocket money. If the food is bad, it's up to the Association to buy food, to look after them properly. Don't assume that their mothers and fathers were able to give them money.'

I watched Katie fight Mira Potkonen in Hungary. It was a close fight, and Katie won it. But Mira was tough. I remember thinking, 'Jesus – she's really improved since I fought her.' But, actually, she hadn't. Today I know: I was a good enough boxer too. But my confidence was on the floor. It wasn't allowed to be anywhere else, other than the floor.

I only had two carded fights in 2014. I also had exhibition fights during the year, but exhibitions don't go down on the card. I fought Deborah O'Reilly, of Olympic Boxing Club, Galway, then Moira McElligott, from Rathkeale Boxing Club in Limerick, and won the Elites – as the national championships were now known – for the fourth time. Moira was a very tricky southpaw, and she hit hard. It was a cagey type of fight. I hurt my shoulder that night over-extending myself on a punch.

Elites Final Night is the best night in Irish boxing; it's class.

The atmosphere is just brilliant.

The boxers march up into the ring and are introduced to the crowd. The national anthem is played. The boxers are absolutely pumped.

The place is wedged; there's no room to move, it's so packed. Your club coach is in your corner, and you've trained in your club in the run-up to this. There'll be a couple of other boxers in the club all training for the same night, and the buzz as the night gets nearer is just electric. The boxers are pushing one another to go harder. Your clubmates and family and friends go to the National Stadium to see you box and to cheer you on. You look around the Stadium and you see so many different club tracksuits. You're seeing people from all over Ireland, from every county. There are people wishing you well, and you're also walking past your opponent's family and teammates. Boxing in that atmosphere is amazing.

I boxed for Ireland again in early 2015. We were up against a team from Ukraine, and I fought Nila Lipska. My club coach, Jimmy Halpin, was in my corner. I'd done a bit of research on Lipska before the fight, and I'd seen that she was a bronze medallist in the Military Games.

'Ah, for fuck sake – do I ever get a bleedin' break?'

She was a bit heavier than me, and very physically there in the ring. But I was able to keep my cool and pick her off. It was the first time I'd fought in the Ireland team in nearly two years, and it was great to be a winner in an all-female team.

But it wasn't a good time.

I was having to organize all the spars myself. I wasn't getting much help, because I was being told that the spars were already there, in Ireland. Today, there are great women boxing at a high level, in loads of clubs around the country. But at that time, it wasn't as good. The standard was much higher in England.

I brought girls over from England, Norway and Denmark, and put them up in my own house. It was awkward, considering I was going to spar with them. There was no escape, for me or for them. I contacted most of them through Facebook: Howyeh, how's it going, do you want to come over and stay in my house and we can do a training camp?

Madness attracts madness, so I knew that the women who accepted the invitation were the sort of people who would, like me, travel anywhere for a good spar.

Valerian Spicer came over from England with her

husband, Laird. We had some great, tough spars; she hit fuckin' hard. Then I went over to hers, two or three times. She was in Islington Boxing Club, in London. I wanted to challenge myself, to get out of my comfort zone; that was where I was going to learn. I asked Corinthians if they'd help with the fare when I was going over to England. I could have paid my own way, but I wanted to feel them out, to see if they actually gave a shit. I wanted to feel appreciated. But they didn't want to help out; they said that any sparring I needed was already in Ireland.

I was thinking, 'Right – if that's the case, I'm out of here.'

It wasn't a row; I didn't fall out with anyone. I just felt that they could have done a bit more. I knew I couldn't get to the top of my game without help; I had to be bossy and pushy.

But I felt bad. I got on well with my coach there, Jimmy Halpin, and I didn't want to leave him; it wasn't Jimmy who wasn't supporting me. I didn't really want to go to another club; it didn't seem to be the answer.

I'd been boxing for nearly a decade. I really enjoyed it, but I was trying to be the best, and it just wasn't happening. I felt that not many people had faith in me as a boxer – or in women's boxing, generally. They thought I was good, but they didn't see how good I could be. Jimmy saw it, but I don't think many others did.

I've always been the driving force behind everything that I do. It can be erratic and all over the place, but I am the one who sets up what I do. But I'd got to the stage where I was seriously thinking about giving up.

9

To be the best, you've got to train with the best.
It was up to me now.

I was telling one of the coaches in St Margaret's Boxing Club, in Glenageary, that I was fed up and thinking of packing it in.

'Come out and join here,' he said. 'You're too good to give up now. You'll box for our club but Jimmy can still do your corner.'

That was how we worked it out. I was happy with the arrangement, although it was a bit of a mad one. It wasn't as if St Margaret's Boxing Club was suddenly sending me to England for spars. But I'd felt under-appreciated where I was. I think the change of scenery did me good too – a new club, but I still had Jimmy in my corner, and the Margaret's coaches were very generous about that. They seemed to believe in me.

I won the Elites with St Margaret's, at 64 kilos, in early 2015, when I beat Kayleigh McCormack. Seeing Jimmy in my corner must have been a bit like seeing the coach of a football club standing on the sideline with a different club. I don't know if it had ever happened before. But there were no ego clashes; no one was saying, 'I won't work with a coach from another club,' or 'I won't coach you if you leave the club.'

I went back to the Ally Pally in June, for the Haringey Box Cup, with Jimmy in my corner. It was a big ring, so there was plenty of room for movement, and in my first fight I was able to pick off Louise Orton, an English girl, really well. Joanne Lambe, from Carrickmacross Boxing Club, was very awkward to fight against; she's very tall. I'd sparred with Joanne before and I knew what to expect, but it was still difficult to beat her.

I faced Lucy Wildheart, a Swedish girl, in the final. She was like a Duracell bunny; she didn't stop coming at me for the whole three rounds. Under that relentless pressure, I really didn't know how I was doing. When the fight was over and I got out of the ring, I was wondering, 'Fuckin' hell – what happened there?' I've seen people getting out of the ring, convinced they've won well when I've just seen them being bashed. But, still, somehow I knew I'd won. I was making good decisions in the ring without being consciously aware of them. I was starting to believe in myself – much more than I used to. I was voted the best female boxer of the tournament.

Five days later I was fighting in Derrylin, in Fermanagh, against a team from Scotland. I'd agreed to take the fight even though my opponent, Gardner Moore, was fighting at 69 kilos. The fight was stopped in the second round. I never fight for stoppages, ever. I hit and move, hit and move. But I wanted to try it this time. I closed her down, walked forward; I fought more, instead of being up on my toes. I was more aggressive, because I was the smaller boxer – I took the space off her. She was heavier than me and if she'd caught me with a punch, she'd have hurt me. She was a long-range fighter, and I knew she wouldn't be fighting me on the inside. So I got in close and took her range from her, so she couldn't land her heavy shots. I rolled under her punches and got in close enough to work my shots to her body. She couldn't respond because I was too close to her. I stopped the fight.

If I'd let it go on, she might have taken my head clean off. I think it's the only time I've fought like that. I felt awful after it. It just wasn't my style of boxing, and I wished that the fight hadn't been stopped. She was very nice and she'd come all the way from Scotland; it felt like her trip hadn't been worth it.

By now, I just had the one job, in St Vincent's, and I was living with Mandy. We always shared whatever we had. It was hard, because I was only working part-time so I could train, but I was able to manage. I'm not flashy; I've never needed to spend much. I put in as many hours as I could, covering shifts, working hours during the week as well as the weekends. It kept me financially stable, and I was able to train.

If I was at work from eight in the morning till two, I'd get out for a twenty-minute run during my break – up around Summerhill and back to work. I'd shower, and finish my shift. I'd go home, chill out for a while, then train later in the day, at my club. I managed the time quite well and made sure I was never chasing my tail; I always had a plan. I was happier when I knew what was ahead; I realized that quite early on, so I always planned my day and my week. I made sure that I could train twice a day, made sure I knew what days I'd be working. I was in control of my time, and I was happy with the balance I had between work and boxing.

When I was working on the weekends and I had a fight coming up, Jimmy would come in to Vincent's during my break. We'd go into the TV room and we'd do pads. Some of the women I work with would be in the room, and they'd sit there, watching us.

'Oh my God – Jaysis –'

'And she's going back up after this to hoover them floors? Where's she getting the energy from?'

I liked the women I worked with, in the household depart-
ment. A lot of them were older than me, and I always felt
good in their company. I loved the chats, the normality of it.
I felt included in that; it made me happy. They were very
funny women, very witty. There was always something going
on; it was like living in an episode of *Fair City* or *EastEnders*.
They'd be going off for their sneaky smoke breaks, dodging
the head of the hospital. They'd turn the corner and – *boom* –
walk straight into him. And they'd come back and tell us
about it, make a story of it. I didn't smoke, but I'd go with
them for the company. When we were walking back in, if we
ran into the head of the hospital, we'd pretend we'd been
doing anything except smoking outside.

'Thanks very much for that! I'll drop that mop up to you –
don't worry!'

The bosses weren't eejits. They knew where we were
after being. They were laughing as well. It was a massive
world away from boxing. And I liked the differences between
the two.

There were Carol and Linda – they're sisters – and Saman-
tha. They covered for me when I was away boxing. I wouldn't
have been able to keep the job if it hadn't been for them. I
was very lucky, and grateful, to have them as colleagues.
There was Sandy too. In catering, there were Martha, Jean-
ette, Seán, Betty, Helen, Mary and Teresa – Mother Teresa;
she's been there as long as the hospital. Martha was one of
the people I'd have been comfortable asking for advice; she
was always very helpful, a good listener. It didn't feel like a
job, sometimes; I was going in to have the craic – and a bit of
cleaning here and there.

Jimmy knew Billy Walsh, who was the head coach of the
High Performance Unit. Boxing is a small enough circle, and

Jimmy had coached Darren Sutherland, who'd won a bronze in the Beijing Olympics. Jimmy talked me up and asked Billy to give me a chance. Jimmy believed in me, and I think he got that across. He persuaded Billy and the other coaches that I was good enough, and that added to my self-belief. Jimmy's word got me in. My hard work and dedication would keep me in. I was going to earn my spot.

Before that, I'd been training in the High Performance Unit at the weekends, with Pete Taylor. It wasn't every weekend; it might be a couple, then he'd be gone for a while. But in 2015, after Jimmy had spoken to Billy, I was let in more regularly, to train. It wasn't on a permanent basis, at first; it was a day here, a day there, or a couple of days in one week.

The High Performance Unit was a massive gym right next to the National Stadium. There were three rings. It was Baltic in the winter – the heaters never worked. At the back of the gym there was a strength and conditioning area. It wasn't state of the art but it was what boxers needed – a weight bench, a squat rack, a spinning bike, medicine balls.

But it wasn't about the building or the facilities. The reason why any boxer would want to be there – why *I* wanted to be there – was because all the top boxers in Ireland were there. I'd have a boxing coach and a strength and conditioning coach; I'd have a nutritionist. They all worked together, to help me to become an all-round athlete, to become the boxer I wanted to be. And there were training plans.

I'd come in on, say, a Tuesday, and I'd start off with a strength and conditioning session. In the afternoon there'd be a boxing session. On the Wednesday morning there'd be a track session and in the afternoon a bag session. Thursday, it might be strength and conditioning again, and a boxing session. There might be sparring on Friday morning, and then home until the following Tuesday. The plan was laid out so I wouldn't be overloading; I wouldn't be doing too much of any one thing. The plan was designed for me – it wasn't just thrown together. It all happened in the one location, and I was getting the rest and recovery between sessions. My body wasn't being burnt out.

And I wasn't dashing off to work, on top of training. I was only working in St Vincent's at the weekends now; I'd have to get used to managing with less money. Basically, I had decided to become a full-time athlete.

I'd been around a good while, and I hadn't been winning international fights. I was twenty-five. I'd decided, 'I'll give it this year and see how it goes.'

It was one of the best decisions I ever made.

I wasn't being paid, and wouldn't be unless I brought home a medal. But I wanted to be there. To be the best, you've got to train with the best.

It was up to me now.

Years ago, people thought that the more training you did and the longer you trained, the fitter you'd get. But today it's all about smart training, doing things correctly, and listening to your body. A good coach can put a plan together for *me*, and listen to *me*. It's about balance, and specific tasks on specific days.

It's all very professional. But at the same time, a good coach is like family. No one gets to give out about my coach in front of me. When I win I give my coaches a hug. I don't actually know what I do when I lose. The coach will always put his hand on my shoulder after a fight, whether I win or lose. He's seen – he *knows* – the work I've put in. He knows the commitments I've made, and the sacrifices. The coaches have seen me on my worst days. I'm very emotional; I'll sometimes break down and I'll have a whinge. I might be feeling that I'm not getting anywhere. They'll see it, and have a chat with me. It's grand; they know me. So, when it comes to me getting into the ring and boxing, they are emotionally attached; they've been with me in the whole run-up to the fight. If I'm winning, it's great; they're getting to see the fruits of what they've been doing – they get to watch that in front of their eyes. But when I'm losing, they're losing with me. Their hearts are breaking, because my heart is breaking – because I'm the one who's in there fighting, and I'm the one who's going to have to get out and deal with the loss. And they know that.

They'll give me a hug.

'It's all right – we'll go again.'

It might be one of the hardest fights and one of the hardest losses I've ever had to deal with, and they'll be trying to help. Words from the coach, and constructive criticism, mean more than any words from someone else. It's an emotional relationship; we've been through the highs and lows together. Club coaches give up their time voluntarily. In a way, it's mad: they're giving away hours of their time every day. But they love the sport and they love helping people; they're watching people grow and change.

When the boxer is in the ring, the coach can't be emotional; he has to stay switched on, to help the boxer get through the fight. When I'm fighting and Noel Burke, my coach at St Mary's Boxing Club, is in my corner, he rarely looks at me. He's looking at the other boxer. He'll throw an eye on me but he's reading my opponent. Great boxers don't necessarily make great coaches, because they don't have the coaching eye. And there are coaches who don't have that eye; they just look at their own boxer.

'Keep your hands up – keep moving!'

But if my opponent's left hand is down, Noel will tell

me to shoot across with my right: 'She's open for it.' Sometimes I can't see what he can see. He'll shout it out; he'll be helping me.

I need to be able to trust my coach. I'm going into the ring to be hit in the head. I could be seriously hurt if I had a coach I didn't trust in my corner. I have to trust that he has my best interests, and that he's smart enough and has enough knowledge to make sure that I don't get hurt. I need to know that if I'm in a fight and I'm being badly hurt, my coach will throw the towel in.

'It's time for her to get out now – she's taken too much punishment.'

I believe that Noel would do that, if he thought he had to. He wouldn't be going, 'Oh, she'll be heartbroken if I throw the towel in.' He'll be thinking, 'She'll be brain-dead if I don't act now – throw that towel in quick.' There are coaches who wouldn't throw the towel in when they should, because of their own ego, and because they're weak; they don't want to upset their boxer.

I like coaches who are honest, who don't sugar-coat things. Sometimes, when a boxer is generally good, the coach won't tell her that she's doing something bad; he'll let her carry on. The coach should be able to step up and say, 'What are you doing?' If the coach isn't doing that, the boxer will never improve. My coach, Noel, will always tell me straight if I'm doing something wrong. If I'm sparring with one of the lads at the club, and if I'm standing with him and try to go toe to toe, Noel will stop the spar, and he'll say to me, 'D'you want to get out? D'you want to get out now? 'Cause that's not boxing.' 'Toe to toe' means just standing and fighting, or looking for a scrap. I'm a technical boxer; I'll hit while I'm on my feet, I'll be moving – hit, and move. I *can* stand and go toe to toe, but it's not how I should be starting a spar. I should only

115

be doing that when I need to. My sparring partner might be bigger than me, and he's going to hit harder than me, a lot harder. Me trying to go toe to toe with him doesn't make sense, and Noel will point that out to me.

'You have to get on your bike – on your feet, moving all the time, popping out the jabs, keeping your head movements.'

He won't let the scrap happen, but others might, because it's good entertainment. But it's about hitting and not getting hit; that's why I'm sparring.

If I'm on the bag, Noel will be calling out combinations and if my techinique isn't right, he'll be calling me up on it.

'That's not a hook – that's not how you throw a hook.'

I do know how to throw a hook, but I often throw bad ones, and Noel doesn't let me away with it. He's making sure that I'm turning my fist into my punches, or lifting my elbow, or turning my hip into it. Anybody can hit a bag but I'm supposed to be hitting the bag correctly, every time. There are coaches who wouldn't challenge me because of what I've achieved, and sometimes there's an assumption that I know everything there is to know about boxing. But Noel will challenge me; he'll tell me when I'm doing something wrong. That, I think, is the key to a good relationship with the coach: I'm not afraid to take criticism off him and he's not afraid to give it.

I'd love to coach, but I don't know if I'd be great at it. I think I'd be a good coach on the floor – I'm good on technique – but when it comes to getting in the corner and having a boxer fighting in the ring, I don't know if I'd be good at that. I don't think I'd be watching the other boxer. I'd be watching my boxer. I'd feel every punch. I get more nervous watching people I know box than I do when I'm boxing, myself. I start not liking boxing when I'm watching a friend, someone I care about.

'Ah, Jesus Christ – I hate this sport.'

I *do* want to coach, but getting up and doing someone's corner – I would have to be coached to do that. Seeing someone being beaten, knowing the work they've done – and I've been there myself – it's almost like a death. We forget about the wins; we'll always remember the loses.

From the very beginning, I knew that I needed a good coach. And, actually, I've never had a bad one. Pete Taylor is a very good coach. I think a lot of the good work he does, he picked up from Zaur Antia, Ireland's head coach. A good coach learns from other coaches. He's open-minded, and picks things up as he watches the other coaches work.

Jimmy Halpin, my coach at Corinthians and Glasnevin, is one of the best in Ireland. And it was Joey O'Brien, my first ever coach, who made me aware that boxing was more than fighting. Paddy Corcoran, Declan Geraghty, Albert Roche – Shane Roche's da – and Dave McGovern, at Corinthians, all helped me to become a boxer; Terry Hamilton and Richard Fox, in Phibsborough Boxing Club, always looked after me when I went up there to spar; they did pads with me, and were very encouraging; Leo Keogh and Paddy Fitz, in Finglas, were legends; Noel Burke, my coach at St Mary's; Gerry Storey – I'm very, very grateful to all of my coaches.

In the High Performance set-up, I was surrounded by good coaches. And I felt welcome. Billy Walsh was the performance director and head coach. Zaur Antia was there, and Eddie Bolger, and John Conlan. I felt I'd been kept away from their professionalism and expertise, but now I was in. Much more was expected of me; they were doing things that weren't possible in a club. The School of Combat, the Tic Tac, the partner work – these things weren't being done in the boxing clubs back then. For me, it was mind-blowing; it felt like a new sport.

Having a strength and conditioning coach, John Cleary, was new. I was like a sponge; I was absorbing everything. I really, really wanted to get better – all the time. I was ready to give it everything, to see how it went.

I was training alongside Michael Conlan. It was like holding a carrot in front of Rudolph. It was just fuckin' brilliant; I loved it. He was the World champion by then; he won it in 2015. I watched him train; I watched what he did.

Michaela Walsh was there with me. Her da, Damien, had often taken training if Pete Taylor wasn't there; this was before I got into the High Performance Unit. I remember thinking when she was a kid, 'This girl's really good.' She was brilliant. Christina Desmond was there too, and Gráinne Walsh; there were other girls who couldn't put as much time in because of work commitments.

Things just started to change. I could concentrate on my boxing. The clubs are fantastic, but a club boxer and an international boxer are two different things. It's the difference in the levels of intensity, and the attention that's given to recovery strategies. If you're working from nine to five and you're going to training from seven o'clock to nine, you're not getting enough recovery time. You're straight back in to work again, and straight back out to training. It's hard. But now I was training twice a day and getting proper rest and recovery between the sessions. I got fitter, and stronger. My body started to change. It got more defined; I had more muscle. The puppy fat came off. I could avail myself of the dietician Sharon Madigan. She was telling me what I should be eating before a session, and after. Sharon was pointing me at the foods I needed to help the muscles grow and repair. She told me which vitamins I needed, because we lose vitamins when we sweat – and boxers sweat a lot.

There was always a good atmosphere in the High Performance Unit. Billy and Eddie would ring clubs around the country, to get sparring partners for their boxers. The sparring partners would come in nervous but, forty minutes in, they'd be at home. The gym would always be busy; there was always a good buzz, a bit of banter around the place.

Later in 2015, I boxed Nancy Moreira, a woman from Cape Verde who was based in Portugal, in Waterford. It was the final of a box cup, in Dungarvan. I was boxing with Glasnevin at this stage. Jimmy had moved there, from Corinthians, and I'd gone with him; it made more sense to be in the same club as my coach. Nancy Moreira had a big height advantage over me. She got into the ring and did the whole dance, from corner to corner to corner. I was like, 'What the fuck is this one doing?' I could see the game in her face; she was up for it. The bell went, and every punch she threw I could see coming from a mile off, because she was throwing with venom. I was able to get my shots off quicker, and get out. It was a great fight, and I was glad to win against an international boxer because the World Championships were coming up the following year.

I finished up the year beating Cheyanne O'Neill in the Elites at the National Stadium. It was a cagey fight. We knew each other – I'd beaten her in Dungarvan and I knew how good she was. It wasn't the most spectacular fight ever. It was the sixth time I'd won the Elites, my first time with Glasnevin.

My Nanny had dementia in her last years. I saw the early signs. Just before her eightieth birthday, I was planning on having a party for her in the house. I spoke to my aunties – my Da's sisters – and they'd noticed it too, that she was forgetting things. Every year, without fail, she'd send all her grandchildren birthday and Christmas cards. I think she'd thirty-nine grandchildren and twelve great-grandchildren at that stage. But she missed my birthday, and Joel's. I was out there with her and she never even said Happy Birthday. I wasn't like, 'Where's the card – where's the spondoolies, like?' But I knew something wasn't right.

She was forgetting things – not *bad* bad, but she'd start to get upset. Then she got ulcers on her legs. She went into the Connolly Hospital in Blanchardstown, and caught MRSA and deteriorated rapidly. The dementia came on tenfold then. She eventually went into a nursing home. She stopped talking. I've never seen someone change so quickly. She picked up these little habits. She had her little handbag and she'd fill it with tissues, spoons and the remote control. Everyone in the nursing home would be going around searching for the remote control and someone would say, 'Try Esther Harrington's bag.'

She died in the nursing home, in August 2017.

10

There were people shouting; I didn't know what it
was, but they weren't shouting for me. It did cross my
mind that I was at a huge disadvantage, fighting a
Kazakh boxer in Kazakhstan. But I blocked it out –
I didn't let the thought take over.

Everything seemed different. I was winning my fights, but it
wasn't just that. I could have taken a loss and bounced back,
because I was surrounded by the right people. I felt that I
was part of the team; I wasn't a token female. I felt like I
belonged. I was happy.

The women were being taken seriously. People had finally
realized that the quality of women's boxing in Ireland – and
outside Ireland – was very high. We were training through
the week, Tuesday to Friday, rather than rocking up on a Saturday or a Sunday, or having a camp now and again; the
women were training with the men and we were being trained
by the same coaches. If the coaches were bringing in a
male team from another country for a training camp, they
brought in a female team as well. We had proper plans, our
weight was being monitored. There was more of a team
spirit amongst the boxers and the coaches. The differences
weren't massive, but they were significant.

In the airport on our way to the 2016 World Championships in Kazakhstan, we were all taking pictures; the craic was
good. There was Ceire Smith, Donna Barr, Dervla Duffy,

Moira McElligott, Gráinne Walsh, Christina Desmond, Katie Taylor and myself. Katie and Ceire had been to the World Championships before, but the rest of us were going for the first time. Everyone seemed happy. We'd been prepared properly. We were ready. Zaur Antia, Eddie Bolger and Gerry Storey were the coaches with us, and Anna Moore was the team manager. Molly Ryan, the physio, was with us too. The physio is a massive part of the team. If you're fighting on successive days and you've picked up a few injuries, the physio is there to help you go on to the next fight. She keeps you in the game. She's also who you go to, to let off a bit of steam.

As part of the preparations, we'd had a training camp in Dublin in May 2016, with the team from France. There was a great buzz around the place. I fought Amina Zidani in a test match at the end of the week. I was fighting at 64 kilos. 2016 was also an Olympic year, and Katie was going to the Worlds to try to qualify for the Olympics, at 60 kilos. I accepted that I was boxing at 64 kilos. It was not an Olympic weight – the next weight up after 60 was 69 – but I had no Olympic ambitions at that stage.

Amina Zidani was a lot smaller than me. She was an aggressive boxer, but it was a smart aggression; it didn't spoil her work. She had real boxing skills behind her. I was fitter than I'd ever been, and I *believed* that I was fitter. I got the decision, and I was made up.

I'd said to myself and to others, 'I'm giving it everything. I'll go out to the Worlds, and whatever happens out there will tell me what's going to happen with my boxing career.'

I didn't have a career, so this experience was going to tell me if I'd have one. It was make or break.

Kazakhstan was an eye-opener of a country. Parts of Astana looked very deprived and other parts looked like pictures of

Dubai that I'd seen. Where we were staying was dusty, like a desert; there was sand and grit in the air. I was going around with my jumper up over my face when I was out; I could feel the dirt in the air, going into my nose and mouth. But it wasn't a massive problem.

Normally, we stay in the same hotel as a lot of the other teams. But I can't remember even one other country being in our hotel in Kazakhstan. They might have been there, but I don't remember – maybe because I was focused on boxing.

The day before my first fight, I was really sick – and I had my period as well.

I was vomiting. I was crying, bawling my eyes out. I was on my knees, getting sick, and Anna Moore was holding my hair back.

'I'm bleedin' *dying* here – what do I do now?'

I'd put all the work in, I was finally getting somewhere, and here I was, wrecked, before I even had my first fight, before I even knew who I'd be fighting.

But Anna was telling me that everything was going to be all right. Anna looked after me. And I was brand new the next day.

The draw was done while this was happening, and the coaches called us all to a meeting so they could tell us who we'd be fighting. They weren't giving us the whole draw, just who we'd be fighting in the first round. Zaur, the head coach, read out the names:

'Kellie, you face the Lithuanian.'

Her name was Austeja Auciute and she came from Donegal! She'd boxed with Finn Valley Boxing Club. I'd come all the way to Kazakhstan to box a girl who'd been living in Ireland until the year before. My stomach was in a bundle; I'd get beaten by an Irish girl in my first fight.

It was strange seeing Billy Walsh with the American team

in the warm-up area. It felt mad. Billy had left the High Performance Unit and gone to coach Team USA in late 2015. I hadn't really had Billy as a coach; I never got a chance to work with him. I had my speaker playing 'The Foggy Dew' and all the rebel songs, and the Americans were playing their rap.

So my first fight was against Austeja – and it was as tough as fuck. There was a lot of pressure, but I was imposing it on myself. I was so nervous, I couldn't breathe properly; it was like there was a layer of cling film across the top of my throat, with a just a little pinprick in it for me to breathe through. She put the pressure on big time; she wanted the fight. I tried to stay calm – but it was hard. She was bobbing and weaving and rolling in, looking to throw big heavy shots. I could read it, and I was able to stay tall and stay in the pocket – stay mid range – and meet her as she came at me.

I won. I was in bits after it, but I'd got through the first fight and some of the pressure was off.

I boxed against Cindy Rogge in the next round – and I knew Cindy too. She'd been at the training camp with the German team in 2013, and we'd sparred together. I became friends with Cindy then, although she didn't speak much English. Another girl on the German team did the translating for us. When I saw I'd been drawn against Cindy, I was like, 'For fuck sake – now I'm boxing a friend of mine.'

The fight was three days after the first one. You've trained for a long, long time and, when you get there, you just want it to be over. I'd three days to think about what might happen, what might go right, what might go wrong. It was a long three days.

Cindy was very technical, and very strong. There was meaning in her punches; she wanted to hurt me. She had a great engine. She didn't rush things, but she worked hard. I knew she wouldn't be wasting her strength or throwing stupid shots. I knew I could afford to get into mid-range distance with her. I was sharp enough to slip her punches when I was in mid range. That was how the fight played out. I stayed at long to mid range. I countered off the shots that she threw, and sometimes just popped the jab out – moving around on the back foot and making her come forward; then back into mid range again, moving the head, so I wasn't being caught. I was in complete control. It was a unanimous decision. I remember feeling really good after winning it.

I was shook when I got the news, the following year, that Cindy had died after an asthma attack. An athlete, and such a strong boxer, and just twenty-three – younger than me. I was really shocked and saddened.

I'd won two fights, and now I'd have a third; this was brand new. And I knew I was going to have to give the next fight the kitchen sink, because I'd be fighting Zarina Tsoloyeva, from Kazakhstan. I'd be fighting the next day and people were saying that it might be taxing on me, so soon after the fight against Cindy. But it wasn't. I'd been in all those box cups, where you fight day after day; I'd done it before and I'd do it again.

Zarina Tsoloyeva was Kazakhstan's golden girl. She looked like a supermodel and there was a lot of white noise around her. I wasn't intimidated, but I was anxious to know what I'd be up against. I just wanted to get into the ring again.

It was a massive arena, packed with people shouting for the local girl. I loved it. I loved walking in, being the underdog. I loved the fact that the thousands there were supporting women's boxing. I'd never experienced anything like this.

There were people shouting; I didn't know what it was, but they weren't shouting for me. It did cross my mind that I was at a huge disadvantage, fighting a Kazakh boxer in Kazakhstan. But I blocked it out – I didn't let the thought take over.

The fight started. She came out at me and she was like glue; she was stuck to me. She never took a backward step. I was exhausted from the first bell, the pressure she was putting me under. There was no let-up; she wanted it so badly and the crowd were pushing her on. She was able to maintain the pressure right through the fight. It's hard to know how you're doing in that kind of situation. I was boxing out of instinct; I didn't have time for thinking. Her hair was coming out of her headguard – she had so much of it! It was a sign that I was landing a lot of shots, because her headguard was being pushed around her head. But I wasn't thinking that. I was just thinking, 'Stop and fix your headguard and give me a fuckin' break.' When the fight was over and the headguards came off, we both looked like we'd been in a war.

Waiting for the decision feels like for ever but it's actually quite quick. I didn't think I'd won, I didn't think I'd lost; I was clueless. But I'm like that after a lot of fights. The coaches knew I'd won – Zaur, Eddie and Gerry.

'Did I get it?'

Zaur was like, 'Very good fight – very good boxing.'

'It was close.'

'Yeah, you got it.'

But I was still thinking, 'Maybe I didn't.'

The referee lifted my hand; I'd got the decision.

I remember asking the coaches, 'Did I get a bronze – am I in the medals now?'

'Yeah, you are – but don't think about that.'

'I'm not, I'm not. But I have – haven't I?'

'Yeah.'

I had my medal in the bag. But I was thinking, 'Don't settle for it.' I don't know how I went from never winning a fight in an international competition to thinking, 'Don't settle for the bronze.' I think it might have been down to the fact that I'd won three fights in a row; my confidence was catching up with my resilience. I'd gone from nearly giving up boxing to being one fight away from the World Championship final.

When I got out of the ring, there were Kazakh broadcasters calling to me.

'Kellie! Kellie!'

I went over.

'You boxed Zarina Tsoloyeva.'

'Yeah, yeah.'

'Good fight.'

'Yeah, it was a very good fight. She's a great boxer – she's very strong. She likes to throw a lot of punches in volume. She came for the fight – she didn't come to give me an easy day.'

'Yes. Do you think she looks like Angelina Jolie?'

I was like, 'Sorry – wha'?'

'Do you think she looks like Angelina Jolie? Many people say she looks like Angelina Jolie – that they could be twins.'

I was like, 'Ahhh, yeah, yeah. That's exactly what I was thinking while I was in there boxing her. "Jesus – this one's the image of Angelina Jolie."'

By now there were two of us in semi-finals – myself and Katie. The rest of the team were supporting us, cheering us on. Over the years, we've learnt how to lose fights, together. One of us might lose, but she'll know that she isn't alone. She can be sad, but around the corner, privately; she is still in the team. We'll talk about the fight – what went wrong, what went right. We'll go over it and come out with positive lessons. We make light of it; we can't change the result. 'Next time . . .'

When your roommate is knocked out of the competition and you're still in, she's very respectful. Your teammates will do anything for you. They almost treat you like you're sick. 'Is there anything I can do for you? Do you want us to get you anything? Do you want anything in the shops? Is everything okay?' That consideration had definitely gone up a level, because the culture had changed. It was more of a team.

I was fighting Sara Kali in the semi-final, two days after I beat Tsoloyeva.

I knew nothing about Kali, except that she came from Canada. The coaches were looking at recordings of her previous fights, coming up with tactics for me. I wasn't there with them; I don't like watching my next opponent on a screen. But Zaur, Gerry and Eddie were analysing Sara Kali's fights.

'What does she do all the time? What is she good at?'

'Right – we need to tell Kellie to try and make her go for the body and when she does that, counter with an uppercut.'

They'd have my tactics worked out. They'd call me in, and show me a clip.

'What do you notice, Kellie?'

It always feels like a test: 'Ah, Jesus – I hope I notice the same thing they noticed. If I don't, they'll be saying, "How the fuck did you get here?"'

So I'm looking.

'She's really tall – and she likes to keep it nice and long. She uses her jab a lot.'

'Yeah – so, this is what we want you to do.'

They give me the tactics and, later, we do a little training session – twenty minutes, thirty minutes – to go over the drill for the next day. In Kazakhstan, it was a light session; I didn't need to sweat because I was boxing at 64 kilos and would have no problem making weight.

This type of preparation was new to me in 2016. I liked being told what to do. I trusted the coaches. I think they were as shocked as I was – more shocked – that I'd got this far.

It was the semi-final, but it was probably the easiest fight of them all. I picked my shots well. The fight was going so well, I didn't need a whole lot of advice from the coaches. She wasn't coming at me. I just had to stay focused – stay in control.

It was another unanimous decision. I was into the final, at my first World Championships. I was over the moon, and the stars. I felt like there were doors opening in front of me. I couldn't be turned away any more.

Gráinne and Tina went off and got their noses pierced. The girls were coming back with boxes of baklava. Dervla Duffy was the baklava queen. I was thinking, 'Fuck – I'm going to get loads of that when I'm finished.'

I was still in competition, and it's a bit of a prison. The room, and across the street to the steakhouse for my food. That was my life. There was a small shopping centre close to the hotel and I went there and wandered around, looking at the bread and the fruit – just to get out of the hotel for a while. I always have my own little kettle with me. I drink tea and stare at the walls. I watch episodes of *Fair City* on my phone. I like hearing the Dublin voices.

I think now, looking back, that I settled for silver. I was happy to be boxing in the final. After four fights, I might have been mentally exhausted. The final was the day after the semi-final with Sara Kali.

I remember seeing Wenlu Yang in the dressing room. She

looked really, really confident, like she belonged there. Billy Walsh's boxer, Jajaira Gonzalez, had fought Wenlu Yang in an earlier round. I was a bit taller than Jajaira Gonzalez and Wenlu Yang was just a bit taller again than me. But her arms were so long – Billy told us that every time the American girl tried to get close, Wenlu Yang would hold her and ruffle her up, and spoil the work. He told us that she was dirty, that if she got in close, she'd hold me and use her height to push my head down; and that she'd swing me around.

But it wasn't an extremely difficult fight. I was constantly thinking on my feet; I wasn't scrapping it out. There were scrappy moments but most of the fight was skilful moments. I made sure she didn't get too close to me; I didn't give her the opportunity to make it dirty. She didn't fight dirty – maybe because I didn't let her.

It was close.

I remember thinking, 'I *could* get this.'

But I also remember thinking, 'Fuck it, I've been in a World final – even if I don't get it.'

I don't know if I cried. I don't think I did. I think I was too tired to cry.

I don't think I settled for silver before the fight. I settled in the ring. I remember the feeling. Before, I'd always wondered how a boxer could settle for silver or bronze, being that close to gold. But I was there, and it happened. It was easy enough to settle. I *was* tired, emotionally. It was a hard fight but I had more in me to give, and I just didn't give it – and I should have.

But I still thought I'd won the fight. And Zaur thought I'd done enough to win it. Even if I thought I'd done enough I shouldn't have settled for that – enough – because I shouldn't have left it in the hands of the judges.

It was a majority decision.

I was gutted, but too tired to really feel it. I remember, too, I was proud. I'd be only the second Irish woman to bring home a medal, and only a handful of Irish boxers, male and female, had ever won medals in the Worlds.

I wasn't thinking that I'd settled then – thinking it in words. I didn't realize it – understand it – until much later, when I had more experience. I understood it two years later, in 2018, at the next World Championships, when I said to myself, 'I'm not fuckin' settling.' I'd been thinking about how I'd felt in 2016, in the final, reliving it, trying to remember if I'd been tired in the corner, between rounds. I'd been physically fine; my breathing had been good. But I hadn't been as focused. I'd been mentally tired more than physically tired.

After the final, Billy Walsh came over and gave me a hug.

'Well done, love. Did you ring Jimmy – do you want my phone to ring Jimmy?'

He was still being Irish, still looking after his own.

Whenever I win something, I always think back to the way I was when I was thirteen or fourteen; me, sitting on the wall of the flats. And there – in Kazakhstan – I did feel proud. All the grief I'd caused my Ma and Da, and now I was making them proud. Back then, they might have thought that I'd stick with the boxing for a couple of weeks. Now I was Number 2 in the world. I couldn't believe it and, in some ways, I still can't.

I was interviewed by RTE after the decision, and I remember saying, 'Next time I come here I'll be taking home the gold.'

I'd been eating in the steakhouse right outside the hotel, because the food in the hotel wasn't great. I had enough money with me this time; I'd learnt from my mistakes. They'd lovely big juicy burgers on the menu. I wouldn't eat anything like that during the competition, but now I was dying for one.

Anna made a promise.

'After the final, I'm bringing you all over to the steakhouse and you're all going to get that burger you wanted.'

And I was like, 'Yeah!'

When I came back to the hotel I was so exhausted – I'd had five fights in seven days, and it was the first time I'd done well, after grinding away for years – I couldn't wash my own hair. I lay on the floor of the bathroom with my head in the shower, and Dervla washed my hair for me. She scrubbed the head off me. Then she got me up and she dried my hair.

'Okay, Kellie – are you ready to go?'

'Dee, I actually – I physically can't. I'm fucked, like. I just think I'm going to lie on the bed for a while.'

'Right – I'll bring you back something.'

So the whole team went off and celebrated me getting to the final. They had their burgers and chips and they were sending me photographs of their food and happy faces. And they brought chips and a burger back to the hotel for me. We stayed up all night, all the team in the room, playing music, eating chocolate and baklava, just having the craic. I'd lost, but they were making light of it, giving one another a bit of stick. They're the best memories.

11

The waitress gave us the menus and asked
us if we'd like a glass of sangria.
We looked at each other.
'Will we have a glass? There's no one here, like.
Fuck it – come on, we'll just have a glass.'

Estelle Mossely was the World champion at 60 kilos; she'd
beaten Katie in the semi-final in Kazakhstan. A few months
later, Mossely came to Ireland with the French team, for a
pre-camp before the Rio Olympics. I was called in to be a
sparring partner for her.

I jumped at the chance.

'A World champion, like? I can't get better experience than
that.'

So I got in and I was sparring with her. It was neck and
neck; there was nothing between the two of us. I wasn't getting battered; I wasn't battering her. It was really, really good.
That was when I thought, 'D'you know what – she's going to
the Olympics, she's World champion. Fuck it, like – let's give
it another lash and see how far I go.'

Noel Burke was doing the corner for the week of the
camp. I'd known Noel a long time. His niece, Aoife Burke, is
a boxer and she was away with us in Hungary, at the European Union Championships, in 2013. And I knew a lot of the
other boxers out of Noel's club, St Mary's in Tallaght. He'd
been in and out of the High Performance Unit at the same

time that I was in and out. He was there for the week when Ireland and France were training together and he seemed to be looking after me all that week; I think John Conlan had asked him to.

I didn't feel panicked in the ring with Mossely. She was the World champion and heading to the Olympics, but Noel, in my corner, was able to keep me calm. I was a silver medallist at the Worlds, but sometimes I felt like an imposter, and that I didn't deserve what I'd achieved. I kept thinking that I'd been lucky to get as far as I'd got. Even today, I have to keep telling myself, 'You can't just have been lucky since 2016.' But I felt it particularly strongly, that imposter syndrome, in 2016, because it was the first time I'd won anything, internationally, after years of nothing, and I think I kept expecting to be found out.

Most boxers have a family member, usually a father or a brother, who brings them to their boxing club for the first time. Most of the people in Ireland I know who've won medals in Worlds or Europeans have had family involvement in boxing. They grew up with the knowledge and the history, and encouragement in the house. I didn't have that. I went to boxing on my own; I was the one who got myself into it. I was encouraged, but there were no connections to boxing in my family. Growing up, I never really knew what the Olympics were, or their significance. Of course I'd heard of the Olympics, and I watched Katie in 2012, and I knew about Michael Carruth – but I never really *knew*.

I followed those Olympics in 2016, and I watched Moselly – and Moselly won the Olympics.

'Jesus – she's after winning. There's no reason why I couldn't do that.'

That was when the Olympics dream kicked in.

*

Soon after I got home from Kazakhstan, I was walking along, at the end of Parnell Street, when I bumped into Eamon Heery, who used to play football for the Dubs – he's a former GAA All Star. His kids were in Corinthians when I was there. I was friendly with them, and helped them out a bit – showed them how to hold their hands up, encouraged them.

'Congratulations,' he said. 'It's great what you've done. I'd love to sponsor you.'

I'd only had one sponsor before, my Da's friend Martin Lawless. So I thought nothing more of it. But Eamon knocked on my parents' door two or three days later, himself and his wife. I was there at the time. They had a Congratulations card for me, in an envelope.

We invited them in.

'No, no – we just wanted to drop this off.'

It was really nice – a lovely gesture. They were telling my parents that I was fantastic and that I'd always been nice to their kids and they just wanted to show their appreciation – something towards getting my gloves, or whatever I needed. And off they went.

I opened the envelope. There was a €500 note in it. I'd never seen a €500 note – I haven't seen one since.

'Da – there's a five-hundred-euro note in the envelope, like.'

I couldn't believe it.

'Let's see.'

I picked it up, out of the card, and there was another one under it.

'Oh my God – there's two of them!'

He hadn't asked for anything in return; he hadn't wanted me to post it on social media, or to turn up anywhere.

'D'you know what – that's just a touch of class.'

It was such a nice thing for someone to have done. I was

very, very grateful. I wonder now what him and his wife think about what's happened. I hope they're happy.

I was still working part-time in St Vincent's and I don't have a lifestyle that demands a lot of money. I wasn't going around in Alexander McQueen or Canada Goose jackets; I'm a 'Penneys, hun' girl. Money was tight sometimes, but Mandy and my Ma and Da were there if I was ever stuck.

I started to get funding as a carded athlete from Sports Ireland in 2017, after I'd won the silver medal. Because I don't have kids or other dependants, it's a reasonable amount. I was delighted when I got the first instalment. I've been able to save – I know that boxing isn't going to last for ever.

The European Championships were in Sofia, Bulgaria, in November 2016. The Irish team was Dervla Duffy, Lauren Hogan, Shauna O'Keefe, Gráinne Walsh, Christina Desmond, Moira McElligott and myself. (Katie had just gone professional, so she wasn't there.) We'd prepared properly; there was a new energy to it. We all felt good. We were buzzing.

The High Performance Unit had moved to Abbotstown. It was immaculate, and still is; it's cleaned every day – there's no smelly-boxer smell in it. We now had five boxing rings, and a state-of-the-art strength and conditioning gym, and a physio room. It wasn't cluttered and I can think more clearly when the place I'm in isn't cluttered. Even the fact that there was a kitchen was brilliant, especially when I was making weight. I could boil my own eggs – and put my own beans in the pot! It was a better set-up than any I'd been in before, in any of the countries I'd been to. It felt that boxing – and women's boxing – was being taken seriously, and was being looked at as one of the country's top sports.

My first fight in Sofia was against Aleksandra Ordina,

from Russia. I didn't know anything about her. Sometimes you draw a Russian and you think, 'Ah, for fuck sake – not the bleedin' Russian.' And that was what I thought this time.

It was a very busy fight. I was changing from orthodox to southpaw, southpaw to orthodox; I was absolutely wrecked by the end of it. But I was able to keep it nice and long: keep Ordina at a distance. She was smaller than me, and coming forward, just trying to throw a jab, and then a big overhand right. I was working long to keep her at a distance, with my jab and my sidestep. There were shots landing, but I thought that my shots were cleaner than hers.

I lost. Genuinely, I thought I should have got the nod, but it was a split decision.

She went on and won the title.

There was a little café around the corner from our hotel; it was called the Brick Café. Most days we had our lunch and dinner there, because the food in our hotel was crap. They'd offer us a free glass of sangria, but we never took it because we were competing. You're not allowed to drink when you're away with the team; it's not negotiable.

After I'd lost that fight, myself and Dervla Duffy, who'd also lost, decided that we'd go down to the Brick Café for something to eat. The waitress gave us the menus and asked us if we'd like a glass of sangria.

We looked at each other.

'Will we have a glass? There's no one here, like. Fuck it – come on, we'll just have a glass.'

Emotionally, we were all over the place.

We had a glass. Then we had another glass. Then we had two double vodkas. And the party started.

I'd cut down on drinking in 2015 – down to almost nothing. I was starting to get looked after properly in the High

Performance Unit. If people were taking me seriously, I needed to take it seriously. I was drinking maybe twice a year, and when I did I'd end up really, really sick. After the World Championships in Kazakhstan, I went out drinking maybe three times. Then I was off the drink, completely, right up to the European Championships in November.

Now, with a few drinks in us, we were getting the locals to get up and dance, and sing. It was great craic – we'd a brilliant night. We were doing the conga, going, 'Shot – shot – shot shot shot!' at a quarter to twelve.

We went back to the hotel, and I was throwing up all night. Dervla was getting sick as well, but she was minding me. I didn't sleep – I couldn't. I'd started to vomit blood.

Mandy had been coming to Bulgaria, to support me. And my Da, who never goes anywhere – he was going to come too; he'd told me after I'd phoned home to tell them that I'd lost the fight. So I was feeling even worse than I would have normally felt. Mandy would end up having to look after me, instead of seeing me box.

The next morning I could barely walk. My stomach was so sore, I couldn't straighten up. I was lying on the bed, and I heard Zaur, Eddie and Dima – Dmitry Dmitruk, another of the coaches – talking outside, in the corridor.

'We want this decision overturned. We need to go down there and get it sorted out.'

I was listening to this – and I couldn't even stand up straight. The tears were flying down my face.

'That's it,' I said to Dervla. 'I'll never be able for this. If I've to box, I'll take one punch and I'll be folded.'

I really felt that I'd let my country down. If the decision was overturned, and I got the opportunity to fight Aleksandra Ordina again, I wouldn't be able to take the second chance. And if I hadn't been drinking, I could have won the

With Nanny Harrington, Grandda and my older brother, Christopher.

At Nanny Harrington's with my parents and my brothers Christopher and Aaron.

I had been expecting a baby sister, but my little brother, Joel, was born on my seventh birthday.

With my friend Robyn at St Vincent's Girls' National School.

My First Holy Communion – a big pay day.

At the first ever national championship tournament to include women, in 2010. I won the tournament, but still it seemed to me that nobody really cared about us (© INPHO/Dan Sheridan).

Things started to change when women were brought into the High Performance Unit: here I am in 2016 with (*from left*) Michaela Walsh, Katie Taylor, Gráinne Walsh, Ceire Smith and Christina Desmond (© INPHO/Morgan Treacy).

With Katie Taylor after I won the 64-kilo silver medal at the 2016 World Championships (© INPHO/Donall Farmer).

At Dublin airport after the 2016 World Championships with my parents – and a girl with a lovely flag (© INPHO/Donall Farmer).

Consoling Shauna O'Keefe after I beat her by split decision at the Elites in 2017, the first time the two of us were competing directly to represent Ireland at 60 kilos (© INPHO/Donall Farmer).

With Mandy at the airport after I won gold at the 2018 World Championships (© INPHO/Morgan Treacy).

I had to pull out of the 2019 European Games, after reaching the semi-final, because of an injured thumb: that's why I don't look very happy on the medal podium (© INPHO/Soenar Chamid).

I beat Caroline Dubois in the final of the Olympic qualifying tournament in 2021 – and went to Tokyo as the top seed at 60 kilos (© INPHO/Dave Winter).

With my coach at St Mary's, Noel Burke, after I qualified for the Olympics.

My opponent in the Olympic final was Beatriz Ferreira – a really good counter-puncher with excellent ring craft – who had won gold at the most recent World Championships, which I'd had to skip because of injury (© INPHO/Bryan Keane).

Afterwards, waiting for the decision, all I knew for sure was that we'd both given a great display of women's boxing (© INPHO/James Crombie).

Celebrating Olympic gold with my coaches Zaur Antia and John Conlan (© INPHO/Bryan Keane).

After I got back to Dublin, the open-top bus went down Portland Row and past the Five Lamps (© INPHO/Laszlo Geczo).

With my brilliant colleagues at St Vincent's Hospital in Fairview.

re-match – and then I'd have been guaranteed at least a bronze medal. It was an embarrassment. I felt so bad.

I was just lying there, and I got a text – from Eddie. He was asking me to come and see him.

'Oh, Jesus Christ, Dervla – there it is. They're telling me I'm going to be fighting later on.'

I was bawling.

'I have to get up – I have to go in to Eddie.'

I tried to make myself look a bit lively. I put on the tracksuit. I threw water on my face.

I went in to Eddie. He looked at me.

'You're not looking great, Kellie.'

'I've been bawling crying, Eddie,' I told him. 'It's just so unfair.'

'All right,' he said. 'You're sparring later on with Yana Alexeyevna.'

They hadn't succeeded in getting the fight overturned. But I was to spar with the Azerbaijani girl, Yana Alexeyevna, who'd beaten Katie Taylor earlier in the year, in the Qualifiers for the Olympics.

'D'you know what, Eddie?' I said. 'I'm just not feeling it today. I've been up all night crying. I'd appreciate it if you could arrange that for tomorrow.'

'Right – you've a day off today. But you're getting back at it tomorrow.'

'All right – thanks, Ed.'

I went back to the room and I told Dervla what had happened. I was still in a bad way.

The next day came, and I wasn't feeling any better. But I got in and sparred – and I sparred brilliantly. I don't know how, or what the hell happened. But that was it: that was the last time I drank alcohol.

I always drank to get drunk. But I didn't miss it. I realized

I didn't need it. I'll be the first one on the dance floor and the first one to sing, but I don't need the drink to push me.

It would be great if you could go straight home after being beaten. When you've been boxing for years, you just don't want to be there after a loss. But for budget reasons, we all travel to and from the competitions on the same flights; there's no flexibility. Often, it depends on *how* you lose, whether you want to go home or stay – and how long you've been away. If you've been away at a training camp and then on to the tournament and you lose on day one and you've another two weeks to go, you just don't want to be there. You're not really of any use to anyone. But you've to put on a face and support the rest of the team – and sometimes that's hard.

I was out, but I went down to the arena and supported my teammates. Christina Desmond won a bronze; she boxed Oksana Trofimova, another Russian, to win it. It was electric; it was absolutely class. We all won at that moment.

Christina should have won the semi-final too, against the French girl, Maily Nicar. It was a split decision and Christina should have got the nod. But getting the medal – it was brilliant. And Christina's a lovely person. I was glad I hadn't got on the plane home early; it was great to be supporting Christina – to be part of that.

After the Europeans, I just thought, 'Now's the time.'

I wanted to go to the Olympics in Tokyo, and there was no 64-kilo category in the Olympics. I'd won a medal in the World Championships, and people were saying, 'Jesus Christ – she's actually good.' And the training set-up had changed for the better. So it was time to try: to see if I could make the Olympic weight – 60 kilos – and maintain it. To see if it suited me. It was all about managing myself, and not letting my weight go up too much. I had to live the life of a full-time athlete, and I had to be restless and relentless in what I was trying to do. Restless, in the sense that I wasn't happy where I was at, and I wanted better. Relentless, in the sense that I was going to do whatever I had to, to get there.

There were other Irish women boxing at 60 kilos. Shauna O'Keefe had boxed at 60 kilos at the European Championships. So the place wasn't mine just because I'd won a medal at the Worlds at 64 kilos and Katie had turned professional. I was going to have to work hard for it. I'd gone from nothing to something, after all those years – Kellie the club boxer to Kellie the Number 2 in the world at 64 kilos. People in the boxing world in Ireland knew who I was now, and there were expectations. So I was going to drop to 60 kilos, and see if I could maintain it.

I still had the same walking weight as I'd had for a few years. When I was boxing at 64 kilos I'd never had to strain to make the weight, because I was naturally less than 64 kilos. Now, to make weight, I'd have to lose the couple of kilos before each fight.

I needed to know if I could make 60 kilos comfortably – and perform at 60 kilos. A lot of boxers lose their fight at the scales. Their battle is making weight. It's one thing making weight, but I had to know if I could perform at that weight. Was I fighting to make weight, or was I making weight to fight? The coaches in the High Performance Unit needed to see it too: they needed to see that I could perform.

Sometimes you get an impression of a person from the way they look, and I always thought, when I saw Noel Burke, 'I wouldn't mess with him.'

When I'd sparred with Mossely, Noel had been very, very

straight, and very detailed in what he was telling me to do – even though I was just there to spar. He was giving me great advice, but not overloading me with too much, just enough for me to take in and use. I thought he was brilliant. As the week went on, I got to know him more, and how he worked. I watched him with one of his boxers from St Mary's, George Bates. I liked the way they worked together. It was very professional.

So I decided to talk to Noel. I was trying to shrug off that feeling of being an imposter and to build up a bit of real self-belief. And I thought that a change in my routine might work if I was going to chase the Olympic dream – something that I'd never thought I'd ever be chasing. I got his number and texted him: I'm thinking of changing clubs. Any chance I could have a chat with you? I was a bit anxious. I didn't know how it would go. Would he think I was a bit mad, too demanding?

I went out to St Mary's and met him. I wasn't sure about the change of club. What if I switched and, a few months later, I realized that it wasn't what I'd wanted? I asked Noel if it would be all right if I came and trained for a while, and then we could make the decision together.

I told him exactly what I wanted: 'Listen – I've won a bleedin' medal but I don't want to be put on a pedestal. I don't want to be Kellie Harrington, World medallist. I want to be just Kellie Harrington. If you're doing pads with some-one, I don't want you to single me out and give me pads. I just want to fit in with everyone. I just want to be one of the gang – that's what I want, like.'

'Listen, Kellie,' he said. 'Sorry to give you a rude awakening – but that's all you would be here, anyway.'

And I was like, 'Oh – okay. Cool.'

And it worked. I joined St Mary's.

*

The Elites final was in early 2017, and I was boxing at 60 kilos. I fought Shauna O'Keefe, who had boxed for Ireland at 60 kilos in the Europeans three months earlier. We were part of the same team; we were friends – and still are. But a little bit of tension had been building in Bulgaria. Shauna had originally boxed at 57 kilos. She'd fought Katie in the Elites at 60 kilos, the previous year – before the Olympics. Shauna boxed at 60 kilos in Bulgaria because Katie had turned professional. Now, I'd made the decision to move down to 60 kilos. I hadn't been going around telling people; I'd kept my cards close to my chest. But there was definitely tension. I think Shauna guessed – with Katie gone – I might be dropping down to 60.

Sport is sport – it's tough. Shauna was – and is – a friend of mine. But there's no room for friendship inside the square ring. There was only one place on the Irish team: sometimes you have to be the predator. And nobody was telling me to stay at 64 kilos.

We got into the ring and did what we had to do. It was a split decision – I won it. After the decision, Shauna was down on her knees, with her head in her hands. She was distraught. I kneeled down beside her and put my arms around her.

'We'll go again.'

It's sport.

I helped her up off the canvas.

That was it.

12

It's the last kilo that's hard. I'm nearly there, but I
have to deprive myself of the simple, leisurely little
things – the croissant, the muffin. What is life
when you can't have a bleedin' scone?

There might be more physical power in men's boxing than in
women's, but I don't think there's much difference in the
boxing itself. Just like in men's boxing, women can hit their
opponent anywhere above the belt – torso and head. Women
wear a chest guard. It's like a sports bra, with protective cups.

A real difference between men's and women's amateur
boxing is that women wear headguards. Men don't – I don't
know why not. I'm happy wearing my headguard. The tem-
ples are exposed – and easier to hit – without the headguard.
There's more clashing of heads in men's boxing, more cuts,
and more knockouts.

When I started boxing, I'd tie my hair back as tight as I
could, pull on the headguard and hope for the best. But my
hair came loose all the time. When you get punched, the
headguard moves, and that shifts your hair and it will come
out from under the headguard. Because of that, a new rule
was brought in, where you had to wear a swimming cap or a
hairnet under the headguard. Most women wear a cloth
swimming cap. They put a plait in their hair, or tie it back
really tight – into the swimming cap, and then the headguard.
I wear a hairnet. I brush my hair back and tie it into a bun at

144

the bottom of my head. I put one hairnet over the bun, then another over my head. I get a lot of stick over it; I look like I'm coming off my shift in McDonald's, straight into the ring. I'm one of the few who uses hairnets, but to me they just make more sense. I get mine in one of the African shops on Moore Street.

When I'm in the corner, just before the start of the fight, the referee will come across and tell me to smile, to check that I have my gumshield in – they're not interested in my happiness! Then the referee will turn my head from side to side, to make sure that I've no earrings in, and to make sure that there's no hair hanging down and that my hair is in a cap or a net. If my hair is hanging loose and I turn my head quickly, I could whip my opponent in the eye and, in the spilt second when she loses her vision, I could get in a couple of punches. So it's important that the hair stays under the headguard.

It's only in recent years, I think, that there's an awareness and appreciation of the fact that women in sport have a menstrual cycle – that it's natural. I make no secret of it, because I'll eat people without salt during my period. Sometimes I can't train; I'm bedbound. If I'm feeling a bit tired, I'll tell my coaches. They're fine; they don't bat an eyelid. Zaur claims that I get my period every week.

I had my period during the World Championships in 2016, and at the Olympics in 2021. It seems to fall every time I'm competing. But I can't not turn up, or say, 'Send in a sub.' I know that paracetamol is the safest drug to take. So I take paracetamol and I pretend: I persuade myself that I'm not in bits, suffering with cramps. It's a 'fake it till you make it' kind of approach. When I have my period and I'm feeling a bit sore, I just get on with it. When I feel really bad, I take the day off and give my body a chance to recover. It stops me for a day and a half. I work my way around it. I know exactly when I'm going to have my period – every twenty-six days, sometimes a day before or after. It can fluctuate when I'm making weight, coming up to a competition, when I'm losing body fat. It's integrated into my training plan. I plan for everything. I become more emotional, and I recognize this. I know when I'm going to start feeling bad enough to go to bed. If my period starts at, say, eight o'clock, I'll still train that morning but I'll skip the session in the afternoon.

I know women who didn't have a period for years, because their body fat was so low. It's not normal for women – or men – to have visibly defined abs. You have to work at it; you don't come out of the womb with a six-pack on you. A woman with a six-pack or a four-pack has very low body fat, and that might put her menstrual cycle out of sync. Also, it's harder for a woman to lose weight around the time of her period. I never really struggled with it until recently – because I'm getting older. If I'm boxing on, say, the 27th and I know that my period is coming on the 25th or the 26th, I know that I'll have to be very strict about my diet, because the weight might not shift as easily as it would do at any other time.

Some female athletes decide to go on the pill, to deal with the menstrual cycle at competitions, so they don't have to worry about cramps and fatigue and emotional upset. But you can put on weight when you go on the pill. I'm happier working around it, working with it. People in sport are more open about the menstual cycle now, but it's still not enough. There are coaches who haven't educated themselves. If I asked for three weeks off because I'm having my period, they'd give me the three weeks off rather than be forced to talk about it. There needs to be more open discussion about what women experience once a month – never mind at competitions – and how challenging and difficult it can be to train, or make weight, or box. The coaches need to be better clued in to it.

We've had female coaches, but they come and they go; they get disheartened because there isn't a lot of support for them. Boxing is a male-dominated sport and, often, women coaches aren't confident in their ability. When I stop boxing, I'd love to stay involved in the sport. I think I could be a good asset to any team. I wouldn't let any man push me around or let him think that he knows more than I do, or that he's more deserving than I am. I wouldn't lack assertiveness; I've had to be assertive. And I've a lot to give back, lots of experience, and not just in boxing – in life. I can help women get mentally stronger, as well as physically stronger and tactically better.

I got the chance to test myself at my new weight against international opposition a few months after the Elites, when there was a round-robin tournament in the National Stadium. Teams from France and Italy came to Dublin to compete. Round-robins are fantastic, because you get two or three fights, regardless of whether you win or lose. There should be more of them. It's where you gain real experience. You might lose, but you get in again a day or two later. They're a great test of stamina and mental strength.

Flora Pili, from France, was okay – not particularly good. But the Italian, Irma Testa, was one of the best boxers in the world. She'd boxed in the Olympics in Rio. She was taller than me; her arms were very long. She didn't inside-fight. She was quite like me, in the sense that she was very technical. But she moved a lot more than me. She changed – orthodox to southpaw – but wasn't as comfortable doing it as I am. She was a back-foot boxer – it was all sidestep, sidestep, jab, in and out – and I saw the fight as a challenge: to try to get close to her and not be chasing her around the ring. When I got close to her and I ended up putting my arms around her, her hands came down over mine and trapped them. I was trying to pull them out, but it was very hard. It suited her; she was wasting time and I was tiring. I remember thinking, 'Fuckin' hell – she's bleedin' dirty.' But she wasn't; she didn't hit any low blows or push my head down. She was smart.

I won on a split decision, and I felt great fighting. I was trying things; I wasn't being overly careful. There was nothing to lose and a lot to gain.

The first tournament I won at 60 kilos was the Nicolae Linca Golden Belt, in Romania – even though I didn't actually make the weight.

It was a three-day tournament. For my first two fights, I'd made the weight both times – 60 kilos on the button. In the final, I was to fight Daria Abramova, the European champion at 60 kilos. By the morning of the final weigh-in, I was hungry, I knew I was overweight, and I'd had enough.

I was rooming with Christina Desmond. 'Look it,' I said. 'I'm not going to make weight. I'm done – I don't care. I'm not training just to make weight.'

'Oh my God, Kellie. Just do it.'

'No – I'm done. I'm not doing it.'

Then I thought of something. I knew that Christina was *under*weight.

'Tina,' I said. 'You weigh in before me. You'll be underweight. So when you weigh in, you look at the scales and say to the two women, "Look, I know I'm underweight but that's still weighing heavy." And when I stand on it, I'll say, "She's right – it *is* weighing heavy. I'm 60.2 there but I'm actually bang on the weight, like."'

I went to the weigh-in with Christina and Carly McNaul.

Carly weighed in. Then Christina followed her, and she was underweight.

'These scales are wrong,' she said. 'I'm lighter than that – it's wrong.'

Then I got on the scales: 60.2 kilos.

'She's right,' I said. 'The scales is wrong. I should be bang on sixty.'

The two women running the weigh-in were confused. But they decided to let me through. We walked out the door. We were laughing and hugging each other.

'*How* did we get away with that?'

I felt like I'd cheated the system. Because if you don't make weight, you're finished – out.

The weight categories are important because heavier boxers have more power behind their shots. If I'm fighting a smaller boxer she'll probably be faster than me. But if I'm going to throw a right hand at her and I let my weight fall onto my back foot, to push back off it, all of my body weight will go into the shot. She won't be able to match that. As well as that, if I want to bully her in the ring and just walk at her, walk her down, my superior weight and size are an advantage; she'll feel my weight. I've often been pushed back by shorter boxers who have more meat on their bones than I have. I've sparred with heavier boxers – women and men – and if they keep coming forward, I can *feel* their weight; it takes the energy out of me. So it's important that I box at the right weight.

It's always a challenge making weight and, since that competition, I've always been up to the challenge. I'm able to go past 'No, I'm not doing it', to 'Okay, I'll do it.'

Daria Abramova had beaten Shauna O'Keefe in the Europeans; she was the 60-kilo European champion. I'd seen that fight, so I knew what she could do. I was half-dreading it, but part of me said, 'Fuck it – I'm here, I'm the World Number Two at sixty-four kilos.'

She was a hitter. She was smaller than me but she could bang.

'This one hits like a bleedin' horse.'

I kept it nice and long, to stay away from her, to try not to get sucked in. I was trying to hit, and get out.

She'd throw three or four hooks in combination. If I got caught, my head was going to be pinging. Everything came from the ground up. She'd shift all of her weight to the right, and push from her right side, up from the ground, up into her hip; all of her body weight was coming with those hooks. They hurt; they could have stunned me. I'd feint, and get close to her, making her think I was going to jump in. She'd throw, but I'd duck back out a little bit. Feint, get her to throw again; sway out and throw a jab; sway out again and throw another jab; sway out, and be gone – don't stay in the pocket. I couldn't take the risk of standing there and trading punches with her.

I could hear Zaur from the corner, telling me what to do. When you're in a fight like that it's great to have someone who's so good at reading fights. Zaur got me through it. I listened to everything he said, and did it – and I beat her. It had worked, and we were delighted. It was a good indication of where I was at, at the new weight. The effort felt worth it.

As far as I'm concerned, Zaur is the best technical coach in the world. He's so good at reading fights. He's great at analysing the opponent and coming up with a strategy to beat her. His plans and programmes are brilliant.

Zaur uses a drill called Tic Tac that involves two boxers. Boxer 1 will throw an eight-punch combination: a straight left, straight right, left hook, right hook, left uppercut, right hook, left hook, right uppercut. Boxer 2 has to block the first punch, slip the second punch, roll under the hook, roll under the other hook, lean back from the uppercut, back in to block the hook, and the other hook, and lean back for the right uppercut.

This drill gets me used to having combinations thrown at me; I become able to block them and evade them, and I practise moving my feet at the same time. Zaur's instructions are very precise and very controlled, and the repetition becomes part of my muscle memory.

Zaur is watching your whole body – your head, your shoulders, your hands, your elbows. He's making sure your hands are closed, your elbows are in, your shoulders are relaxed, your chin is tucked in; where your legs are positioned, where your weight is positioned; are you forward too much, are you back too much; when you throw the jab, are you dropping the right hand; are you jumping in with it?

There are so many little things that he sees that others don't; he really is a perfectionist. His English wasn't great when he arrived from Georgia, but he knew how to demonstrate what he wanted physically. His English is good now, but he still demonstrates while he speaks. He stands back and watches us.

'Hey! Don't lean in – don't put your head forward – keep your hands closed.'

If our technique isn't looking as sharp as it should be, he'll stop us – 'This is it' – and he'll show us again, exactly, what he wants: how to move the hip, how far the foot should twist around.

He'll be looking at us, and all the other coaches will be looking too. His eye is amazing. Most coaches don't get the credit they deserve, but it's not every coach that's producing Olympians; Zaur fine-tunes talented boxers coming out of the clubs and produces Olympians. I don't think he gets the credit he deserves in Ireland. He's given his all to Irish boxing.

He's a boxing man, through and through – boxing, boxing, boxing, 24/7. If you're not in the mood to talk about boxing and you see Zaur's name coming up on your phone, you don't answer the phone. Sometimes I have to get away from it; it's not healthy for a boxer to be living and breathing boxing every hour of every day. It might be different for coaches, because they're not climbing into the ring to get the heads slapped off them.

Daria Abramova was quite sour after the result was announced. When I lose, I take it hard. But I'd never be disrespectful to an opponent. If they beat me, they beat me. You shake hands, even give them a hug, and walk off. My big thought after a fight is, 'The fight's over, thank God we're both all right.' It's a strange one, but I'd never want to physically hurt someone. It's contradictory: if I can drop them with a body shot, happy days. But I wouldn't want to hurt someone badly. It had been a good bout, but Daria Abramova didn't get up on the podium to collect her medal.

I was set on my way.

'I *am* sixty, and I'm staying at sixty.'

It's the last kilo that's hard. I'm nearly there, but I have to deprive myself of the simple, leisurely little things – the croissant, the muffin. What is life when you can't have a bleedin' scone?

About two months before a competition, I start to get stricter with my diet. I cut down on the biscuits, I cut out takeaways. No chocolate bars, no cake. I'm really looking after what's going into my body. What I put in, I'm going to burn off. I need to put in what is going to last me for a proper training session. Pasta, potatoes. I need the carbs if my body is going to function properly. I have potatoes cut into chips, then baked in the oven. They take for ever to cook, but I fool myself into thinking that I'm eating proper chips. I eat a lot of vegetables, turkey burgers, chicken and salmon – sometimes. I hate salmon, but I know it's good for me. Four weeks out of competition time, I get stricter still. Breakfast first thing in the morning – a big bowl of porridge, two slices of toast and an egg, a pint of water and two cups of tea. Lunch is at twelve, and I have my dinner at three or four – early. I've more time to burn it off during the rest of the day. Six o'clock is the latest I'd eat. If I have a training session after my dinner, I'll have a recovery shake – powdered carbohydrates – and a bit of protein, maybe a turkey burger. I have two kiwis before bed; they help me sleep. I don't need to kill myself to make weight; I do it the right way. But it's always the last kilo that's the struggle to get off.

The day before I get in the ring to box, I'll be 1.5 kilos overweight. It's nearly always the same. If I'm boxing on a Saturday and it's Friday, I'll be 61.5 kilos. I'd hope to be around 61.2 or 3. The day before the weigh-in, I'll have had a big breakfast and a big lunch – bigger than normal – because I won't be having a dinner. I'll do a training session. I'll be sweating in the session, because I'll wear an extra top or a jacket; I'll have a good sweat. I'll check my weight; I'll be about 60.4 kilos. I can figure out if I can eat, or how much. Most times, I'll have my recovery shake, made with 250 millilitres of water.

When I wake up the next morning, the day of the fight, I just have to feel my belly to know that I'm on weight, or very close to it. I *know*. I'll weigh in, then I'll go and have my usual breakfast, the porridge, the eggs, two croissants – they're my treat when I'm away – and I don't feel that precise weight any more. I feel more normal, once I get the breakfast into me.

The strength and conditioning coach, John Cleary, measures my body fat percentage with a calipers – my triceps, abs, biceps, quads, calves. The nutritionist organizes blood tests, to make sure that everything is all right. When you're sweating to make weight, you lose a lot of minerals, particularly iron, so I'm making sure that what I eat compensates for what I've been losing.

It's a battle when you're making weight. But I think I go about it the right way. I'm eating three meals a day, and I'm still eating snacks – just not the snacks I want. I'm not starving myself, but I'm starving my brain of the nice things; I'm not letting my mind decide that the perfect life is all coffee and muffins and singing 'Kumbaya'. I'm a bit of a diva when I'm making weight, but – actually – it's not too hard.

The European Union Championships were in Cascia, in Italy. It was going to be my first major test at 60 kilos.

I knew the type of fighter that the Polish girl, Kinga Szlachcic, was. I knew she was going to give me trouble and put the pressure on. I didn't box well – the first fight is always the hardest one to get through. But I got the job done. I was through to the next round.

Carly McNaul was there with me, and Dervla Duffy, Gráinne Walsh, Christina Desmond, Kristina O'Hara and Michaela Walsh. Muireann Harte, the physio, was with us. All of us were carrying little niggles – shoulders, elbows, wrists – and Muireann kept us fine-tuned.

Two days after beating Szlachcic, I was in against Ditte Frostholm, from Denmark. It was a good, technical fight and I was comfortable thoughout. I was happy enough with how I was boxing, and happy, too, that I'd made the right decision moving down to 60 kilos. I was having no problem making weight, although that might have been down to the heat; it was roasting in Cascia in early September. The food was fantastic, and I was eating all around me, but I still made weight every time.

Now I was up against Irma Testa, for the second time in four months. Irma was the golden girl here: I was fighting an Italian in Italy. It's hard to imagine that there would be a big audience for boxing in a place like Cascia; it's full of beautiful old churches and the local saint is St Rita. But all of the Italian team were shouting for Irma; it was wild. I beat her well; I was quite shocked. It wasn't easy, but it was easier than the first time. This fight meant much more, but I was in control. I was able to judge my distance and range well; I just felt great.

I was in the final.

I'd boxed Mira Potkonen before, at the Golden Girl Box Cup in Sweden, more than four years earlier, in 2013. Since then, she'd put Katie Taylor out of the Rio Olympics. I knew that she'd beaten her last opponent well, and the one before that – the referee had stopped the fight. I was excited, but nervous too. I knew what to expect, but when it happened: 'Ah, Jaysis Christ!'

It was brilliant.

I gave her a boxing lesson in the first round, an actual boxing lesson. She was edgy, constantly moving; she'd rush at me, throwing three or four punches. But I was making her miss and I was countering her, really cleanly – beautifully. I was making her miss and making her pay.

Halfway through the second round – there were still four two-minute rounds in women's boxing back then – I lost momentum. I was given a standing count. 'One, two . . .' I didn't deserve the count. I was wondering, 'What the fuck is that for? That's a fuckin' joke.' It was for nothing; I was really annoyed. Then I got another standing count, and this time I deserved it. She'd caught me with a big right hand. I was a bit all over the place after that. I wasn't rattled; I wasn't seeing stars. But I was a bit emotional.

'I'm after getting two standing counts!'

I started to panic. When you panic, your breathing is heavier, you become tired, you can't think properly.

It was a split decision at the end – but she'd won, and I knew it. She deserved it.

Mira Potkonen is brilliant; I've always admired her. I look at her and I think, 'There's a role model, that's someone to look up to.' She'd beaten me fair and square. I was nearly telling her, 'Thanks very much for beating me, it was a pleasure to share the ring with you, how's your ma, is your da working?' She's a great boxer, but her presence was so impressive too, just the way she carried herself. When I saw her around the place at tournaments, she looked dominant. She wasn't technically great, but what she had – her physicality and fitness – she put to great use.

I had another silver medal, and I'd lost fair and square to a boxer I admired – but I was devastated. I'd been so close. At the same time, I was thinking, 'Howyis, I'm here now – this is me and I'm not going anywhere.' And the big lesson I took home with me was that I'd stay calm the next time. I wouldn't panic.

Michaela Walsh won the gold fighting at 54 kilos, and Gráinne Walsh won a bronze at 69 kilos. There was a great buzz in the team after it was all done. We all went out for a pizza.

'We're in Italy – the pizza's going to be great.'

We were at Bernard Dunne, the High Performance Director: 'Ah now, Bernard – we've a few medals here now. Time to put your hand in your pocket.'

When we were walking back to the hotel, a big outdoor

stage had been set up in one of the town's squares. There was a DJ playing music. No one was allowed onto the stage, but we were like, 'Come on – fuck it, we'll get up.' Muireann was with us, and Christina's da and Gráinne's da. We all got up on the stage and we were dancing, and people coming out of the restaurants and cafés were dancing. Then the police arrived and were trying to get us down. We weren't budging but, eventually, we had to get down. It was a lovely moment. We were a bunch of girls having a great time, without a drop of alcohol.

13

She wasn't the better boxer. I'd been unlucky.
I remember thinking it at the time: 'I'm getting
closer.' And I also remember thinking, 'That's it,
like – no more respect.' The respect would have
to stay outside the ring.

It's one thing loving a scrap, but doing everything to back that up – that's the challenge. You need to be fit; you need a good engine. The scrapper doesn't really think about technique; she just wants to close down the distance, get stuck in and throw millions of punches and stop the fight early on, if she can. A technical boxer will have a good shot selection. She's trying to see the punches before they even get thrown – she's reading the fight. If there's a left coming, she'll slip back out of its way. I'll see a punch coming, and I'll move with it; the punch could be right in front of my face, but it hasn't landed because I'm riding the punch – I'm moving with it. If a scrapper gets into the ring with a woman who boxes like me – who's more technical, who picks her punches – the scrapper will need to be very fit, or she'll burn out after one round, just coming forward. The technical boxer will taunt her and pick her off. The technical boxer has to be even fitter. She's constantly on her toes; she's being pushed back and pushed back, all the time.

People are labelled scrappers or technical boxers and, a lot of the time, they're being mislabelled. Someone is called a scrapper and she starts to think she's a scrapper, and she loses her boxing ability because she starts to believe that she's made for scrapping. She becomes the label – the wrong one.

I've seen it happen.

'Oh, she loves to fight – she loves a good tear-up.'

And I've seen the opposite, too. I've seen women who've realized that they're not just a label, a scrapper; they're more than what they've been told they are.

I was never a scrapper. I was a technical boxer from the start. But I like to put myself into scrappy situations when I'm sparring – to get more comfortable in the uncomfortable. Then, if I come up against an opponent who's going to be dirty and aggressive, who's going to come forward looking for a fight, I've prepared for that. But there's also a danger. I could start thinking, 'Well, I've been doing that in training, I've been standing toe to toe with such-and-such, she's been banging shots and I've been banging shots back and I've been able to hold my own, so I'm going to be well able for this one here.' But I shouldn't be thinking that way. I'm a technical boxer; that's how I box. If I think I've won the first and second rounds, I'm not afraid to have a bit of a tear-up in the third. But, really, it's not what I should be doing. I don't need to be doing it, and I'm also getting hit. Why would I want to be hit?

For that matter, why did I get into the ring in the first place? I came from a family with three brothers, and we used to bash each other – or, more accurately, I used to bash them. They'd give as good as they got, and I loved it – the adrenaline. It was competition; it was great. I knew I could fight; I knew I was good at it. I was good at having a scrap and I decided to transfer it over, into a sport. Just at a time when I badly needed something. And no one in the house ever said, 'Girls don't fight.'

*

The Europeans were coming up in early 2018, and then there'd be the World Championships later in the year. They were my short-term goals. The Olympic Qualifiers would be in early March 2020.

That was the goal: the Olympics.

But I parked it. I didn't think too far ahead; I just concentrated on the little things that would get me there. I was training full-time and getting a lot more fights. I was in the mix; I had two silver medals, and I'd been boxing for a year at 60 kilos. But I tried to avoid talking about the Olympics. I'd try to keep it inside me until I'd booked my flight to Tokyo. Toyko was the goal, but if I didn't do well in the Worlds, if I didn't get through the Qualifiers the following year, there'd be no Tokyo. I'd be going to the Europeans and the Worlds knowing that whoever I fought, I was likely to come up against them again on the road to Tokyo, or in Tokyo itself. So my focus was on the tournaments in 2018.

We'd been building the culture since Bernard Dunne had come in as High Performance Director: if I performed well, the rest would follow. If I performed well and lost in a good fight, it was nothing to be ashamed of. Just perform well – that was what I was trying to instil in myself. 'Performance is key, performance is key – I'm going out here to perform. Whatever happens happens. Concentrate on performance.'

I fought Amy Broadhurst in the National Stadium in February 2018, for my eighth Elites – my second at 60 kilos. Amy was a very good underage boxer; a lot was expected of her. I had to beat her if I was going to go to the Worlds, because only the national champions qualified to go. This was the first step.

In March, we went to the USA, a full Irish team – women and men. It was like a round-robin tournament, and each fight was in a different city in Massachusetts – Boston, Springfield, then Manchester. I hadn't been to the USA before, so I was really excited to be going. It was freezing. It was snowing so hard one day, we weren't able to travel to the next city.

We were training while we were there, too. There was a great sense of togetherness; we were a team, in the USA to perform. There were three of us on the team from the same club, St Mary's – George Bates, Aoife Burke and myself.

I had three fights. I fought Stacia Suttles twice, and Amelia Moore once. I beat Stacia both times, and was beaten by Amelia – a split decision. I lost concentration that day; I let America distract me. I was a tourist, rambling around, not doing what I normally do before I fight. We were allowed pick our music for when we walked out to the ring, because it was a show and – I suppose – because it was America. I'd never done that before. I picked a dance song, 'You Got Me Baby'. I was buzzing, nearly dancing, as I went to the ring. I just wasn't focused. That was the last time I let myself be distracted before a fight.

When the boxing was all done, we were let go shopping. We were brought to a mall full of the big outlets. The amount of stuff that everyone got was mad, because everything was dirt cheap. It was Gucci at Penneys prices. Normally, I hate spending money on designer clothes – 'Nope, I'm not spending it' – but here I was, 'This is fuckin' brilliant – I'll take that, I'll take that, I'll take two of them.' I got three pairs of Levi jeans, a Tommy Hilfiger jacket, five Levi's tops; I got a couple of belts, a Gucci bag and Gucci jeans. I let myself go.

The European Championships were in Sofia again, and my first fight was against a girl from the Czech republic, Kateřina Humlová.

We were on opposite sides of the warm-up area, waiting to go, looking across at each other. I was ready, prepared for battle, when everything shut down. There'd been a power cut.

I took a breath – I was ready to burst with frustration. Just before a fight, I'm always going, 'I can't wait till this is over, I can't wait till this is over.' Now I was being forced to wait.

But I walked away and took my vest off – I was sweating, and wanted to stay nice and cool – and I started to do a bit of yoga.

The coaches would have expected me to get worked up: 'I'm ready to go!' But I just thought, 'What's the point, like? I'm only going to burn myself out.' So I decided to find a corner, stay calm, and do the yoga; the fight was going to happen whenever it happened. I was stretching, breathing – trying to relax and not let the delay become an anxiety; trying not to think about what could go right or go wrong when we did eventually fight; trying to keep myself in the now.

While I was doing the yoga, Kateřina Humlová was trying to stay warm; she was standing up, sitting down. She was very restless, and she was looking across at me, wondering what I was up to.

I'd started doing yoga a few months before, just to be doing something different. Michael Darragh MacAuley, the Dublin footballer, had recommended it to me. Michael works for Dublin City Council in the north inner city. We met through his work with the local youth and became good friends. Boxing can be very stressful, and I'd wanted to try something that would help me stay calm.

The power came back and I was getting warm again, loosening up, and I was trying to smile and laugh and have the craic. Zaur and Dima had never seen me like that before a fight. I think they were pleasantly shocked.

I got in and I boxed, and it was a handy enough fight. She was tall and very rangy, but I was able to pick my shots. I was very comfortable.

Two days later, I fought Yulia Tsyplakova, from Ukraine. I'd seen her box before. She moved a lot; she bobbed and weaved and kept slip-slipping, constantly moving her head, and always moving in, breaking down the distance, trying to take my space from me. But I could move back and sidestep, and shift – move my right foot to my right side, drop my left shoulder, switch feet, move my left foot to where my right foot was, then throw a backhand or a hook. It was a close fight but I was landing the cleaner shots; she was just rushing in. I'd have kicked up murder if I hadn't won it. But I did win and that meant I'd be fighting Mira Potkonen again, for a place in the final.

I felt ready.

I'd been hoping I'd meet her, but later, in the final. I get better the further I go in a tournament. But still, I was ready. In a short space of time I'd gone from being the boxer who was delighted to win two fights in a row to the boxer who hoped to meet the best European boxer in my weight category in a final.

I felt confident. She'd a great engine, but I wasn't worried that I wouldn't be able to match it. I wasn't afraid, and she knew it.

It was a close fight, but she won – a split decision. Looking back, I think I was still giving her a little too much respect. But we felt – me and the coaches – that I should have got the nod. I don't think it was unfair; I wasn't going to argue about it. I took it on the chin, and that was it. I had a bronze. I was happy enough – because I hadn't settled for it. I'd settled for silver in Kazakhstan, but not this time. I'd wanted to beat her; I'd tried to beat her. The decision was the decision.

There was nothing more I could have done. She wasn't the better boxer. I'd been unlucky. I remember thinking it at the time, 'I'm getting closer.' And I also remember thinking, 'That's it, like – no more respect.' The respect would have to stay outside the ring.

There was one more tournament before the Worlds, a multi-nations in Romania, in September.

I fought Jelena Jelic, fighting for Serbia, in the first round. She was smaller than me, and a real tidy boxer. It was tough, because it was my first fight in the tournament – what I'd call a rusty fight. I was blowing – breathing heavily – by the end of it, and tired. But I'd got the job done.

My next fight was against Yulia Tsyplakova, who I'd beaten three months before in the Europeans. She won this fight on a split decision – but I should have won it on a unanimous one. It was clearer than the last time I'd fought her. Our physio, Séamus Caffrey, had helped her with her facial injuries, enough to let her fight against me, because a Romanian boxer, Cristina Cosma, had really punished her in her previous fight. Her eye was badly swollen and she had a cut right over it. Séamus had taken the swelling down, but she still looked like she'd taken a battering – even before we got into the ring.

She was as shocked as I was when she got the decision. She was overjoyed, like she'd won the World Championship – and I was bleedin' gutted. I got down out of the ring, gathered up my stuff, and went outside.

I don't think I'm a sore loser. It's not nice, but you can learn from a loss. You learn nothing from a win; nobody goes back over a win with you. But a loss – you go over and over and over it again, alone and with your coaches. I don't like it, but it's educational. You learn, and the skin gets thicker.

That time, though, it just seemed so unfair.

I was sitting under a tree, crying, and John Conlan came out after me.

'What the fuck are you crying for? This is only preparation. This is experience – what else did you come here for?'

He was right. I was hurt, but he was dead right. It was preparation for the World Championships. I'd dust myself off and get going again.

I started drinking coffee that day. I'd been making weight, but now I didn't have to. We all went to Starbucks and I got a coffee with loads of cream in it, and sugar and all the syrup. It wasn't the coffee, really; it was everything on top of it. I felt like I was part of the gang, drinking the coffee. It was, literally, the first time I ever drank coffee. Eventually, I weaned myself off the sugary stuff, and now it's just a flat white – no sugar.

I was happy with the way things were going. I was sparring well, and taking instructions from the coaches. I'd a variety of sparring partners; we were trying to replicate the styles of possible opponents coming up in the Worlds – long range, shorter and more explosive, southpaws, orthodox. I was improving.

It's contradictory, I know, but I'd always had the 'Fuck it' approach to my boxing career. I'd made the decision, 'It's all or nothing,' in 2015. But after that, it was, 'Fuck it – whatever happens, happens.' I tried to take the pressure off myself that way. I tried not to think, 'I have to win, I have to win.' I made it into, 'If I win, I win – if I don't, I go again.' I'm aware of my contradictions: my confidence and lack of confidence; my anxiety and 'We'll see how it goes'; my ambition to win the Olympics and my 'Fuck it – whatever happens, happens' attitude. But I think the contradictions were pulling me in the same direction. I had them working for me.

My approach has had to change a bit since then. I go into tournaments now knowing that – as far as all of my possible opponents are concerned – I'm the one to beat. They're training to beat *me*. This means that I can't just say 'Fuck it' any more. There's an expectation that wasn't there before. If I'm drawn against someone really good, I can't just go, 'Ah, Jesus Christ, I'm after drawing *her*.' I have to go, 'D'you know what – she's after drawing *me*. She's good but I'm fuckin' better.' I have to trick my way into the right frame of mind. I act my way into the feeling. I'm faking it till I'm making it. I'm still learning as I go along.

But it's inevitable: I will be beaten. Knowing that – living in the real world – takes some of the pressure off. It's two women in the ring throwing punches at each other and one of them is going to lose and, sooner or later, it's going to be me. Every dog has her day.

I do my best. I prepare as well as I possibly can. I hate losing, but hating something and being afraid of something – they are two different things. I'm not afraid of losing. It's a very lonely place when you *do* lose. When you win a fight, there'll be seven hundred messages on your phone; when you lose, there'll be four or five – Mandy, a few cousins, my best friend, and my Ma. And that's another thing I know: there's life outside of sport, and I have my family and the other people I love.

14

It was over. We were both gassed, done – exhausted.
I went back to the corner. The gloves came off,
the headguard came off.
'Did I get it?'
'It's very close.'

The first thing was the smoke in the air. I'd been in hotter places, but the air was so thick – and the people were everywhere; I'd never seen such crowds. The roads were so busy – no lanes, no lines. And people were coming right up to the windows of the bus, trying to get us to buy all kinds of things – teddy bears, chains, mad things.

We pulled in to the hotel. It was like a palace – unbelievable. There were restaurants, shops, hair salons. Outside, everything seemed run-down. Inside, everything was luxurious.

I'd brought a couple of white builders' masks with me, because I'd read that the air in India was likely to be smoggy. I was a bit self-conscious wearing them outside. But I wasn't there to fit in, or to stand out, and I thought they'd help me breathe properly.

After we sorted out our stuff in the hotel, we all went for a walk. There were kids with no shoes, begging, and stray dogs everywhere. And I saw a pair of vultures, and a monkey. We were passing by what looked like an army barracks, and the monkey was just walking out the gate and stood there – and walked back in.

After that, I didn't really leave the hotel unless it was to train or compete. I wasn't going to be a tourist. There was a walk that I did, up and around the side streets near the hotel – but that was it.

I loved the food – the dal, the naan bread. I couldn't eat the plates of cakes they put out for breakfast. I'd brought my own porridge with me, and my own raisins. But I queued every morning for an omelette – the nicest omelettes I ever had. I was checking my weight about eight times a day, but I had no problem making weight.

We were told not to brush our teeth with the water from the taps, so myself and Gráinne Walsh – we were sharing – were taking trays of bottled water off the trollies in the corridor. For my first fight, Dima had Delhi belly, so an American coach had to do my corner, with Zaur. Dima thought he was actually dying, but a couple of cans of Coke sorted him out.

My first fight was against Troy Garton, from New Zealand. I didn't know her. As usual for me in the first fight of a competition, it was challenging. From the bell, she came forward. She was smaller than me, and she had both hands high – so it was hard to get through her guard; I couldn't catch her. She stuck to me; she tried to smother my work, to stop me.

When I'm under that kind of pressure, I never know how the fight is going; I've no awareness of winning or losing. But I knew I was being tested, big time. I was able to keep her off me as she came forward, and I was able to land more shots than she did. When the fight was over, and I'd won, I was glad that I'd had that kind of fight, at that stage in the competition. It wasn't that they were going to get easier, but it was good that the first had been hard. I felt good coming out of it.

I'd made weight, I'd won my first fight – a lot of the worry was gone.

There was a gym in the hotel and we'd go down there in the mid-afternoon, most days, and I'd do a very light sweat/pad session. A long-sleeved top and a pair of leggings was all I needed to get a sweat going. The gym was full of boxers – boxers on the treadmills, boxers skipping. There was a pool outside, and there were boxers doing pads and skipping beside the pool. But I don't think I saw anyone *in* the pool.

My next fight was two days later, against the Indian boxer, Laishram Sarita Devi. She was older than me and she'd been a World champion.

'I've come all this way, to India – to fight an Indian. This is brilliant.'

The arena – the Indira Gandhi Sport Complex – was huge; it was absolutely class. They'd filled the place with school-kids, which was great. The day I was fighting, Mary Kom – the best boxer in India, who'd won eight World Championship medals – was there too, boxing. The place was rocking – electric. I was pumped. I was the underdog, and it was great. I was saying to myself, 'I'm going to show yis.'

Every time I landed a shot, the kids screamed. Every time Devi landed a shot, they screamed. It was hard-hitting, it was technical. It was everything that the crowd could have wanted. I caught her with a shot from a southpaw stance, straight on the chin. She went down. I was shocked when it happened. It was brilliant – the crowd went, 'Oooh – !' She got back up, but it had rocked her. She was smiling at me, taunting me, and I was smiling back at her. She was sticking her tongue out at me and I was laughing back.

We were both wrecked after it, but elated too – because it had been a great fight.

I was buzzing heading back to the corner, to get my gloves and headguard off.

'How did it go?' I was asking the coaches.

'It was a close fight.'

I went back to the middle of the ring. I was asking myself, '*Was* it a close fight, or did I win it – or wha'?' I really didn't know.

It was agony, because the announcer was speaking in Hindi first, then English.

'And the winner, by a split decision . . .'

'It'll go to the home girl,' I thought.

But it was me – I'd won. It was very close, but I'd won. I'd beaten the Indian, in India.

The whole place erupted. But there was no hostility. They'd been cheering for the local, and by the end of the fight they were applauding me because it had been a great fight.

I was now boxing for a medal.

I'd fought Caroline Veyre, the Canadian, before, in a Box Cup in Dungarvan. I knew I'd have my work cut out, because the last fight had been a split decision. I liked Caroline's style of boxing. She was a smaller fighter, but she wasn't someone who just comes in close and smothers the other boxer's work. She'd get in close, but not so close that she couldn't throw shots. She'd get to mid range, and she could bang – she hit hard. There was good volume in her punches, and she had a good shot selection. She threw from all different angles and she was good at cutting the ring off too. I was in for a hard night's work.

I like to fight people who I've never fought before. I don't get as nervous. I just go in and box. But you have to fight whoever's put in front of you.

It was a tough fight. If I hadn't had the fight, four days before, against Troy Garton, it might have had a different outcome. But the fight with Troy really warmed me up for the fight with Caroline. It was a pressure fight, but I knew that if I'd survived the last one, I was going to get through this one.

I kept it as long as I could, and kept moving. If she broke me down, she'd go to work and she wouldn't stop working. She was selective in what she threw; she didn't waste energy on punches that weren't going to land. If she got close to me and I stood there and tried to throw, she'd just slip my punches and work into my body and up to my head, and then roll back out and go again. I had to keep her long, make her throw – and counter, and move again.

I'd been in this position two years before, in Kazakhstan, fighting for a medal in the Worlds. Back then, nothing had been expected of me. This time it felt no different. I wasn't letting myself get caught up in the razzamatazz and the hype. It's one of the reasons I keep myself to myself at tournaments. I stay away from the hype; I don't believe in it. And I don't want to create any hype, in case I do start believing in it. I just concentrated on the boxer in front of me.

Caroline was a good boxer. She was just unlucky to be in the wrong weight class. She dropped down to 57 kilos after the Worlds.

It was a unanimous decision. I had a bronze medal.

'Who's next?'

Karina Ibragimova, from Kazakhstan, was a southpaw. She was tall – taller than me – and rangy. But I was really in the rhythm. I boxed really, really well. I felt great in the ring. She'd no answer for anything I did, and I'd an answer for everything she did. Every shot she threw, I countered her with absolutely everything. This time I knew I was winning. I felt it, and it didn't feel dangerous, anything to be wary of.

Keeping your concentration for the nine minutes is very hard – but I wasn't going to switch off. I do it, sometimes, in sparring; I lose concentration. But this was a fight, a semi-final, and I wasn't going to let my concentration slip for even a split second – because that split second could be the one when I end up getting sparked out and hurt. I stayed focused – on myself, and what I was doing.

'Out to the centre – move your head, move your head.'

When I'm moving, I'm on my toes. On my toes, I'm able to think. I'm light, I'm on my feet, I'm moving – I'm thinking. If I plant my feet, I stop thinking – or I'm over-thinking. I've lost it. It becomes a scrap. I'm being caught, I start to put my hands up, and I start taking punches on the gloves or on my arms. They're not landing, they're not hurting – but that's not what the judges are thinking. Or the people outside the ring – they're just seeing me holding my hands up. 'She's hurt – she can't defend, she can't throw back.' When I'm sparring I might hold my hands up; I'll take big shots, to try and give two back. I shouldn't be doing it. It comes down to concentration.

I felt great when it was over.

'Fuckin' hell – I'm in my second World final. This is abso-lutely mental.'

But – still – I wondered how it was possible, how I was in India competing at this level. Was it just luck? I genuinely wondered if it was. 'I'm just fuckin' lucky. I was on the easy side of the draw.' I tried to block out the doubts. But doubt always creeps in when you're boxing nearly every day in a World Championship. The yoga helped, and breathing – and thinking about my breathing, thinking about nothing else – helped. And I pushed back the doubts. 'I got the easy side of the draw – there *is* no easy side of the draw.'

It was brilliant – the atmosphere was brilliant.

There were two days between the semi-final and the final, and the day after the semi – the free day – there was a trip organized to the Taj Mahal. I didn't go. I didn't want to be sitting on a bus for most of the day. I wanted to concentrate on the job I still had to do.

I'd be boxing Sudaporn Seesondee, from Thailand, in the final. She'd boxed Mira Potkonen in an earlier round, and she'd beaten her well. I'd fought Mira three times, and I'd never beaten her. Mira was strong and gutsy. But she'd taken a couple of standing counts against Sudaporn Seesondee.

So I knew that Sudaporn Seesondee was going to be a banger. The coaches were telling me to keep it long, not to stay in close with her; get in, and get back out.

That was what I did.

I lost the first round. Zaur told me when I went back to the corner. She'd landed more punches, and I was probably a bit hesitant – slow to go in, in case I got pinged by one of her heavy shots. Zaur and Dima were calm and relaxed, and they were able to talk me through what I was to do, to go out and take back the fight in the second and third rounds. And I remember thinking, 'Fuck this – I'm going to give it everything.' I remembered how I'd felt the last time I'd been in this situation. I'd fight it out, give it everything; I wasn't settling.

I went back out – it was a different fight. I changed to southpaw, and I kept changing back – southpaw, orthodox, southpaw, orthodox. She was missing with a lot of her shots; I was moving out of the way. I've seen clips of the fight since, and it looks like I was slipping and moving really well – but I might just have been trying to get out of there. I look like I'm out of *The Matrix*, but it was the survival instinct kicking in. But I was surviving successfully. There was so much weight in her punches, she was nearly flying off the canvas – but they weren't landing. I was being more forceful than I had been in the first round. I kept switching – southpaw, orthodox, in, and back out. I had to think fast, I had to think sharp; I had to get in quickly, and get out just as quickly.

If I don't get out, I'll get caught. But as I get out, if I can move – it's as if I don't have bones at the base of my back. I get in, and back out and, as I'm moving, I make sure that I stay out of danger.

I don't remember if I felt that I'd won the second round. I think the coaches told me that it was one apiece.

It was all down to the third round. I was up for it. I wasn't thinking about Kazakhstan now. I was thinking about this fight, these last three minutes.

'I have to give it everything here.'

It's amazing what you can think when you're tired.

'Even if I lose, I want to know that I did give it everything.'

It wasn't war; it wasn't that kind of fight – we weren't battering each other. We gave it all, in a tactical way – in the way that we boxed. But she started to rush her work, just a bit. She left herself open to be caught. She was worried, I think, maybe panicking; she knew it was slipping away from her. She was taking shots and missing shots. It was very close, though.

It was over. We were both gassed, done – exhausted. I went back to the corner. The gloves came off, the headguard came off.

'Did I get it?'

'It's very close.'

I went back to the centre of the ring.

I heard the announcement.

'In a split decision—'

I was thinking, 'Fuck – not again. It's happening again, I'm going to lose it on a split decision.'

'In the *blue* corner – !'

My hand was lifted, but still I looked down at my vest, to check the colour.

'It's me! I won!'

I dashed over to the corner and gave Zaur and Dima a hug. It was a three–two split decision.

I looked up, to see if I could find the girls in the crowd. I saw Gráinne bawling, and screaming like a four-year-old.

I remember walking out when it was over. The anti-doping chaperone was following me. She'd spoken to Zaur when I was getting out of the ring. She would stay with me until I was ready to go to the toilet. It was her job to follow me, not the other way around, so I was able to do what I wanted until I was ready. This is standard protocol when you reach a podium position in a championship; I wasn't surprised that I was going to be tested.

I got changed, got my tracksuit on, so I could go to the medal ceremony. I was just so relieved – relieved, much more than elated.

I bumped into Dima when I was coming back out of the dressing room.

'Thanks, Dima,' I said.

'For what?'

'For all the work you've done. Today wouldn't have been possible without you and Zaur – and Noel, and all the other coaches.'

'The fuck, Kellie! Don't say things like that! Thank *you* – this is every coach's dream.'

The tears were flying down my face.

I got the medal. I was on the podium, in this huge arena, as the Irish flag was being lifted and the national anthem was playing. It was brilliant – it was unreal.

I did the doping test after the medal ceremony; then I went back to the hotel. This time I had the energy to wash my own hair. There was a lot of texting going on: Right, Bernard, where are we going? There was a Hard Rock Café about twenty-five minutes away from the hotel. We had burgers and chips – in India! It was great – the craic was ninety. I'd been in a Hard Rock once before, but here, in New Delhi, the waiters were dancing. It was a show – it was deadly. We were all up dancing too. It was the perfect way to end a perfect tournament.

The Irish women's hockey team had won a silver medal in their World Cup, in 2018. There was a parade for them, down Dame Street. I came into town – little fan-girl – to see them. The street was packed and there was a stage on College Green; Shane Ross, the Minister for Sport, was up there with them.

When I came back from the World Championships with a gold medal a few months later, there was nothing arranged. So Dublin City Council and the Mayor at the time, Niall Ring, had a little homecoming for me, on Seán McDermott Street. Niall Ring called out the Minister for Sport for not being there.

I had a great time. This was my part of the city; I was with everyone I knew. All the patients from work came; it was just brilliant.

About nine months later, the Minister for Sport invited me for dinner in Leinster House. Really, I didn't want to go.

'I don't want to go to fuckin' dinner with him – for what? Because he forgot to say congratulatons to me? What would we talk about?'

But people from Sport Ireland advised me to go.

'I'll go if Bernard and Zaur and Rachael Mulligan go with me.' Rachael was the High Performance Manager.

So they all came with me, to dinner in the Dáil. It was nice, really; we were chatting away. I was sitting to the left of Shane Ross, and Zaur was sitting to his right. I'd asked Zaur to come with me because, coming from Georgia, I thought he'd like to see Leinster House – all the razzamatazz.

We were done, we'd had the dinner, and we were walking out.

Zaur pulled me aside. 'When is the Minister for Sport coming?'

'Wha'?'

'The Minister for Sport – when is he going to come?'

'You just fuckin' sat beside him for the whole dinner.'

'What the fuck, Kellie – why didn't you tell me this was him!'

'Well, like – I just thought you'd have picked up on it. It's no wonder boxing gets fuck-all.'

15

I had an X-ray; nothing came up. Another X-ray –
nothing. But the thumb didn't feel right. I couldn't
move it. I was like, 'What *is* wrong with me?'
My confidence was on the floor.

The Elites were in February 2019, three months after the
Worlds. I wanted to box in front of the home crowd, after
coming home with the gold medal, but I had no one to fight.
It just happened that there was no one out there to box me.
It happens, sometimes. One year, there'll be millions of girls
in a weight class; the next year there'll be no one. It's haphaz-
ard. It's the story of women in sport, really. But it's improving,
in boxing. There's a better structure, and more opportunities
to get started in competition – Under 18s, Under 22s.

The IABA paid for Jelena Jelic, who was now based in
Sweden, to come to Dublin to fight me on the night. In the
second and third rounds, all I could think about was my
hand. It was sore; something wasn't right. I won the fight,
but as soon as the glove came off, I felt my hand – and I just
went, 'Oh my God – what's that?'

I thought I'd dislocated my thumb.

I texted Julianne Ryan, a physio I knew who was in the
Stadium that night, and asked her to come down and have a
look at it.

It was the thumb on my right hand, and Julianne was moving it around. It was loose, and she was like, 'Yeah, okay – don't

panic. You've probably dislocated it. And there could be a bit of a fracture there, Kellie. So look – don't worry about it, don't be panicking.'

I was ready to die.

Julianne advised me to go and get it checked. So I went to St Michael's Hospital, in Dun Laoghaire, at eight o'clock the next morning. I wasn't able to drive, so Mandy brought me. They referred me on to St Vincent's Hospital, in Merrion, and I got the X-ray, which confirmed that I'd both dislocated and broken the thumb.

I was like, 'Oh, Jesus Christ.'

'You're going to need an operation.'

I was devastated.

'That's it – that's me done now. No Olympics – gone.'

I was finished; my whole boxing career was finished. I hadn't needed to fight Jelena Jelic. It had been my decision. So I was pissed off with myself; I was very, very upset. Everything that I'd worked for was – in my head – gone.

There was still a bit over a year until the first set of Olympic Qualifiers, in March 2020 in London. But first I'd be six weeks out of training. Then I'd need another six weeks to build the thumb back up, and get ready. Twelve weeks – three months – is a lot of time when you're training to qualify for the Olympic Games.

After my initial overreaction, I tried to be positive. It was bad news, but it wasn't *that* bad.

'Fuck it – d'you know what? I'll be back, I'll be ready to rock soon enough.'

I had an operation on the thumb a week after. I'd never had surgery before; I'd never had a serious injury. It was keyhole surgery, so I was in and out in half a day. Kieran O'Shea was the surgeon.

I remember being pushed along the hospital corridors,

and being wheeled into a small room – before being brought into the operating theatre.

The anaesthetist and the nurses were lovely.

'I want you to count backwards from ten.'

I was thinking, 'That's not going to knock me out.'

I woke up, and it was all over.

'Where's my tea and toast? I'm starving.'

I'd been told that the tea and toast was great after surgery. And it was.

I couldn't train. My hand was in a cast. I'd gone from training one hundred per cent, right down to zero. I started to question myself.

'Who the fuck am I – what am I doing?'

I'd so much time to fill. I couldn't work. Normally, when I had time off boxing, when I wasn't in competition, I'd put in extra shifts at the hospital. But not this time.

The European Games were coming up in late June, in Minsk – in Belarus. I'd never been at a European Games – it's like a mini-Olympics, for all sports. So I was thinking, 'I'm going there – that's my goal.' My hand was healed – so I thought – and I got back to training.

The last training camp before the European Games was in Belfast. I hadn't gone to the little multi-nations competitions that I'd normally have done to be ready for Minsk. So I had my final preparation in Belfast, with a team from India, and Team USA. The thumb felt okay. I felt fit. But I wasn't under any pressure; I wasn't throwing my hands the way I normally would in a fight. So I wasn't really tested before we flew out to Minsk.

My first fight was against Irma Testa. I'd fought her before, but this was a different kind of fight. She was more aggressive than she had been before; she came forward more. But I won the fight, and the hand felt grand after it.

Next I fought Agnes Alexiusson, from Sweden, and I won. After I got back to the changing room, and the adrenaline came down, I began to feel a twinge in my thumb – the same thumb.

I think I probably caught her with a slap – instead of turning the hook inwards, I caught her head with the thumb.

It wasn't as painful as the last time, because I hadn't dislocated it. But it *was* sore – shooting-pain sore.

The physio, Lorcan McGee, and the team doctor, Jim Clover, were looking at it.

'I don't know if I'm actually just thinking it . . .'

The thumb was swollen, and it was getting more painful.

I was in the final and I didn't want to miss it, so I started banging in anti-inflammatories. The pain eased a bit.

'It can't be broken.'

But I couldn't hit pads with it.

'I think I need to get an X-ray on this, before the final.'

I was due to fight Mira Potkonen, and I didn't want to be going in one-handed and getting the head punched off me. I had a CT scan, and Jim and Lorcan saw it. It seemed to show a bit of a fracture, but they weren't sure if it was the old one or a new one. I was still hoping it wasn't a fracture at all.

Jim and Lorcan went to Bernard and, together, they made the decision to pull me out of the final. I was thinking, 'Jesus, I've let them pull me out of a European Games final. Am I losing my bottle – chickening out?'

I was confused. I genuinely thought I hadn't broken my thumb. I was going around with my hand in a splint, just to keep the thumb in place. But I was laced out of it on the painkillers, and convinced that I'd let them withdraw me from the final when my hand was all right.

I came home to Dublin and had an MRI. Nothing showed up.

'Oh my God – I've thrown a possible European title away.'

I had an X-ray; nothing came up. Another X-ray – nothing. But the thumb didn't feel right. I couldn't move it. I was like, 'What *is* wrong with me?' My confidence was on the floor.

The consultant in St Vincent's, Kieran O'Shea, told me that I needed another CT scan. So I had the scan. I was expecting Kieran to give me the all-clear. I'd already started work on the hand, exercises to build the muscle up.

But he sits me down.

I sat down.

'Look, Kellie – I'm very sorry to tell you, but your thumb is worse than it was the first time.'

I was bawling – crying.

'I'm so sorry, Kellie.'

It felt like he was telling me that someone was after dying. I was like, 'It's all over!'

I was blubbering away, blowing my nose. Then I was, 'Right, okay – when am I getting my operation?'

'Tomorrow.'

'Brilliant.'

I was delighted. I asked him would I be able to go to the World Championships in October, and he told me I would. But I think he just wanted to get me out of there. Someone else could be the bearer of that bad news; he'd had enough for one day.

It was a more complicated operation than the first one. This time, they cut the thumb muscle and flipped the skin over. I was under general anaesthetic, out cold. They put screws in my hand to keep the thumb in place. I had the cast on for ages, nearly for the whole of 2019.

I was out of training. Even going for a run was a problem – the heart rate would increase, the blood would start pumping, then it's coming out through the stitches.

I was a bit lost. I'd been training for the Olympics since 2016; I'd given it everything. Then breaking my thumb, twice – my head was in the gutter.

I started going to yoga again, with a broken hand. It was Michael Darragh MacAuley's idea. It looked odd but I didn't care. I needed to do it for my mental health; I'd have spiralled out of control without it. I went to Yogahub, on Camden Street, nearly every morning. I'd get the bus in, because I couldn't drive. I'd meet Michael and we'd do the yoga together. He was a massive help to me.

It gave my day a shape. I'd be up really early in the morning and getting the bus into town, with my yoga mat on my back, for the seven o'clock class. I'd meet Michael outside the Yogahub, or he'd be inside ahead of me and he'd hold a spot for my mat.

The sessions went on till eight. The last five minutes were *savasana* – resting – where you just lay on the ground and relaxed. That was the best part of it. I'd be chilled out, in the middle of town, hearing the seagulls and the men working outside. It was just a really nice feeling. We'd go to the café across the street, the Cracked Nut, and have a bowl of porridge or eggs on toast, and we'd talk for another hour. If Michael wasn't with me I'd meet another friend, Jessica, and we'd go for a coffee. I would have been completely lost if I hadn't had that, at that time.

I enrolled in a sports psychology course at IADT, the Institute of Art, Design and Technology; the lecturer was Olivia Hurley. I never did the exams or handed in anything, but just being part of that class was a massive help to me. It was something else for me to do, a bit of routine. And I was hearing things that were useful to me.

After yoga and the café, I'd walk around town. I love people-watching. Seeing them going to work, wondering what they worked at, what their lives were like. Around Stephen's Green, across to George's Street – I'd walk to my Ma's, then back into town and the bus back home, or I'd get the DART and Mandy would collect me from the station in the evening. Otherwise I'd have been at home, eating cake all day – and I wouldn't be able to burn it off. So I had to eat the cake in my Ma's instead – and walked it off, by calling up to my cousin Shaunagh's. That was it for at least six weeks.

I have a spinning bike at home, and I was able to start using it about four weeks after the operation, because I didn't have to move my hand while I was on it, or grip the handle-bars. I was sweating to death on it. Another two or three weeks and I was back to very light training. I couldn't punch on my right side, so I did paddle-work. The paddle is like a lollipop lady's lollipop, but the circle is smaller, the size of someone's head. It got me back punching, and moving – I wasn't putting the hand under any strain. And it got the joints going – loosened them.

I was doing strength and conditioning too. I couldn't do a lot on my right side, because of the hand – picking up a weight could have damaged it again – so I was working on the left side of my body, with a dumb-bell. If you're working on your left side you get a natural crossover, a benefit, to your right side – the physio, Lorcan, told me that. I wouldn't be whacking the weights out of it every day, because I'd have ended up like Popeye. But it was great to be working, and great to be back in the gym, in that environment – it was absolutely brilliant. I felt like I was a boxer again.

Then I got back into Tic Tac, a drill where Boxer 1 throws a specific combination and Boxer 2 has to evade it. It's very controlled – there's no contact.

It was all about strengthening my hand and getting fit again – *ring* fit. You can be very fit from running and hitting the bags. But once you step in there between the ropes and someone is throwing digs at you, you're trying to think, you're trying to move, you're trying to defend and you're trying to react – you're trying to survive. You won't be ring fit unless you spend time in the ring. We were trying to get that ring fitness back, slowly. It was a combination of the paddles, then Tic Tac, and then School of Combat, which is more open and involves more contact. The two boxers are allowed to hit each other with the left hand only; then one is allowed to throw the left hand and the other boxer is allowed to throw the back hand. Then one boxer is allowed to throw anything they want, but going forward, while the other is allowed to throw anything, but going backwards. It's fairly open but still controlled. The instructions are given to you at the start of every round.

After about three weeks of the more controlled work, I was allowed to spar. The coaches were looking at me, to see how the hand was holding up and how I was getting on. And they were happy enough. I was grand, but I was really, really conscious of it. I was thinking, 'This can't happen again. If it does happen again I'm definitely out.'

By October I was ninety per cent – almost back to normal – but I missed out on the World Championships. I wasn't ready and I knew it was for the best. But I was starting to panic. The Olympic Qualifiers were in March. I worried that I was missing out on preparation. And I worried that I wouldn't get the strength back into my hand.

In February 2020, we went to Sofia for the Strandja, the last preparation tournament I took part in before the Qualifiers. I had four fights in four days, and I got to the final. I was boxing well. I was happy that I wasn't too far off the mark, and happier still that I'd had the four fights and hadn't broken my thumb again.

My opponent in the final was – again – Mira Potkonen.

The first time I boxed her was in 2013. It was close, it could have gone either way – she got the decision. The second time was in the final of the European Union Championships, in 2017. It was my first tournament boxing at 60 kilos. I won the first round but the next three, I died a death – I got battered from pillar to post. I lost the fight on a split decision. I don't know where the 'split' came from; I lost it. The third time was in the European Championships, in 2018. It was *so* close. I didn't get it, but I wouldn't have argued with the decision – fair dues to her.

So this was the fourth time. I knew she'd edge her way forward; she'd be on her feet and jittery, constantly feinting – but showing it. She wouldn't stop moving. She'd – *bump!* – rush at me, and fire shots. I knew what to expect. But this time I had no respect for her; I was determined to win the fight. I wasn't feeling privileged to be in the ring with her; I knew I could beat her.

Everything that I thought would happen, happened. Except this time, my game plan was different. I was meeting her as she came at me. I was stronger than I'd been when I'd fought her before. I was changing from orthodox to southpaw, southpaw to orthodox – and from the southpaw stance, I caught her with a couple of left hands into the body, and hurt her. I could see it; she slowed down. I threw the same punch, again, and again. They were clear shots. I was in control for the whole fight.

I beat her – and I beat her fairly well. I felt good. Then they called a split decision and I thought, 'Ah, come on – Jesus Christ, it's not a split, I'm after beating her.'

They gave it to her; she'd won. I was devastated. I'd beaten her – convincingly beaten her.

I tipped her glove and got out of the ring. I was crying. And I knew by the look on her face, she knew – and I knew it by the look on her coaches' faces.

My coaches knew too. Everyone was upset. Zaur was ready to flip the lid. I felt good, in that I knew I'd beaten her. But I felt robbed. In the warm-up area, afterwards, I realized that it wasn't Mira's fault. I went across to her and shook hands with her.

I was very conscious of my hand right throughout the tournament. I was constantly thinking, 'Is this going to be the third time – is it going happen again?' But it felt good, it felt strong. I was icing it – immersing both hands in a bucket full of ice for ten minutes after every fight. I'd see the physio after every fight too, after every training session.

Just before the Olympic Qualifiers, we went out to a camp in Assisi, in Italy. We were going to go straight from there to the Qualifiers in London. We were supposed to be in Italy for ten days, but the Covid thing started to happen in the north, in Lombardy, and we had to leave after four days. There were teams from India, Italy, Russia, France, and a couple of Croatian boxers. We were all to have been sparring one another. But we had to go back to our own countries.

Covid didn't feel like a real thing to me, at that stage. I thought it would blow over, and I think the others felt the same way.

We finished off our last bit of preparation in Abbotstown. I'd only had one spar in Italy. I didn't feel ready for the

Qualifiers. I didn't feel confident. I was still playing catch-up. I'd been due to get five spars in Italy but I only got one.

Everything else was being cancelled. Concerts, football – everything. And yet the boxing was still going ahead. I was thinking, 'They're going to pull it any day.' But no – we were on the plane and we were over there, in London.

There were people getting Covid, but the draw went ahead. I was set to box against Aneta Rygielska, from Poland, on St Patrick's Day.

In London, the rumours were flying.

'Two Turks were tested positive.'

Myself and Christina Desmond were roommates. Christina had boxed, and lost – at 69 kilos – on the 15th. We were both confused, a bit all over the place.

'When is this going to get called off? 'Cause it's getting called off.'

'No, it's going ahead.'

Mentally, I wasn't there. I was concentrating on everything except boxing.

On the 16th, I went over to the boxing venue to do a sweat session. This is where you train to sweat a bit of water out of you, to dehydrate, so you can weigh in the next day. After the session, I was hungry – and thirsty. Christina was there too, to support the rest of us, and she was on the shuttle bus with me back to the hotel – I think Carly McNaul was with us too – when the bus driver said, 'All right, love – so you're all off to the airport in the morning?'

I was like, 'Shut up, like – it's not funny. Don't be joking like that. I'm starving, I'm thirsty. I'm not in the humour for it right now.'

But he was like, 'I wasn't lying to you, love – you're going in the morning.'

'Ah, Jaysis – what's he talking about?'

'Were you not told?'

'Told what?'

'Jesus Christ,' he said. 'I've opened my big mouth.'

At that moment, there were still bouts going on, but according to the driver the decision had been made to postpone the rest of the tournament.

I was like, 'This is a bleedin' joke – I need to know for sure.'

Back at the hotel with Christina, I rang Rachael Mulligan, the High Performance Manager, to find out what the story was. I was thinking, 'If the tournament's not going ahead, I'm going to eat.'

'Kellie,' she said, 'we wanted to sit you all down, as a team, and tell you ourselves, not have other people tell you. We still have two boxers in the tournament today and we have to be mindful of that, until they're finished. So please don't tell anybody else.'

I only told Christina, and my club coach, and my Ma and Da – and everyone in Ireland!

To be honest, I was relieved. I didn't feel ready. If the Qualifiers had gone ahead then, I don't think I'd be an Olympic champion today. I might have beaten Aneta Rygielska, but then I'd have had to box against Maïva Hamadouche, from France. She's an ex-professional, with twenty-one fights and seventeen KOs. I just wasn't in the right headspace to be going in and fighting her.

I'd a packet of Cadbury's Turkish Delight Eggs that someone had brought for me from Australia, and I'd been holding on to them for ages. I was waiting till I'd finished boxing. As soon as I was off the phone with Rachael, I was like, 'Right – there you go, Tina, get them into you.'

We were stuffing our faces with chocolate.

16

My sport – my profession – was on hold but
I was able to get back to my job, and it's not a job
that can be done from home. You can't clean
a hospital toilet from your kitchen.
'There yis go, lads – I cleaned the toilet!'

We came home on 17th March, St Patrick's Day. Everything was closed, the streets were empty.

It wasn't clear what was going to happen with the Olympics. I was thinking, 'The Olympics are going ahead, a bit late – in another three months we'll be in the Qualifiers again.'

I took a couple of days off, to assess myself and to think about what had just happened. Then I got back to training, at home. I have a little gym at the side of the house. I have an Air Assault bike; it's hard going. I've my own weights, my own bench, my own squat rack. I'd be listening to music: Andrea Bocelli, Disney, a bit of '90s, a bit of Luke Kelly and Christy Moore.

Mandy held pads for me. She had stopped boxing, but she was doing a bit of coaching in the local boxing club. We'd do pads twice a week.

A week after I came back to Dublin, it was announced that the Olympics would not take place in 2020. No new date was set, but the official statement said that the Games would happen 'not later than summer 2021'. And then a week after that, they announced the games would happen in late July and early August 2021. There was no clarity, yet, about qualifying.

I rang the hospital and told them I was back.

'If you need me, give me a shout.'

'Can you come in?'

'Yeah – no problem.'

So I went in. I was working five days one week, four days the next, for three months straight. I had a permit to drive to work, as an essential worker. And I was training at home.

Lockdown was great – for me. When I'm training I don't have much of a life. I felt I had more of a life during lockdown. I'd go to work, and I'd bring my speaker in with me. I'd be getting the ladies – the staff – up to dance to TikTok dances, during the lunchbreaks. Because there was no boxing going on, the European Boxing Federation was running a shadow-boxing competition. So I said to myself, 'I'm going to win that.'

I made a video. At work.

I walk in with my green work coat on. All the girls are sitting down. I take off my work coat; I'm wearing a top and work bottoms. One girl is walking around with a piece of cardboard: 'Round One'. Someone else comes out with the milk jug, and goes, 'Ding ding ding.' And I start shadow-boxing, to 'We Will Rock You', as the women clap and slap the table to the beat. We rehearsed it for a few days and then we recorded it. And we won!

We started doing little exercises, around the back of the hospital, where they all have their sneaky cigarettes. They'd be having their smokes and I'd bring out the speaker.

'Are yis right – are yis ready?'

And I'd stick on Tina Turner – 'Proud Mary'. And we'd be

walking around the tree, singing along with Tina. *'Rollin', rollin','* in a psychiatric hospital, *'rollin' on a riv-er'*. Work kept me sane.

Shadow-boxing is boxing drills, basically – no gloves, equipment or bags needed. It's more effective than hitting a bag, but only if you have a coach. I've seen kids shadow-boxing and no one's looking at them; the coaches are off having a chat. It seems harmless, but they pick up bad habits. A coach can show you how to throw six punches and tell you to shadow-box for three minutes with those punches. A lot of the time, when boxers are looking in the mirror at themselves shadow-boxing, they don't know what they're looking at. They're just looking at the mirror, banging out a couple of combinations. They're not asking themselves, 'Where's my guard?', 'Where are my feet?'; they're just seeing how good they look shadow-boxing. But all the same it's a very underrated technique. When my hand was injured, it was all I could do; I couldn't hit anything. My coaches, Noel and Zaur, watched me as I shadow-boxed.

'Keep your hands up there.'

'Move your feet a little bit more – you're staying too static on the ground.'

They'd call out combinations: 'One, two – slip back hand. One, two – lean back hand. Back hand – lean back, back hand.'

It made me think more, and I was getting faster, even though I was alone in the ring.

My sport – my profession – was on hold but I was able to get back to my job, and it's not a job that can be done from home. You can't clean a hospital toilet from your kitchen.

'There yis go, lads – I cleaned the toilet!'

I was busy at work, so I didn't think too much about how long the lockdown was going to go on for. I was exposed, but I was very careful. I was *so* careful – washing my hands all the time, wearing the mask and gloves – that I worried about how I'd be when we started to come out of Covid. I worried that I'd end up more vulnerable to the common cold or flu.

But I knew that I was working around very vulnerable people. I was worried about the patients on my ward – saddened for them, more than worried. Everything shut down for them. They weren't getting out of the ward. They weren't getting any visitors. On St Mary's Ward, where I usually worked, there were nine patients. They had a big sitting room, a little dining room, a small smoking area with a window that only opened slightly. Normally, they'd have been able to go down to the garage at the bottom of the Richmond Road for a cup of tea or coffee, or they could go and get their hair done in the Chinese hairdresser's in Ballybough. But they weren't getting out, at all.

I worked on the isolation ward. If a patient came in, they went into isolation, where they were tested for Covid. If they tested negative, they were sent on to St Louise's Ward. There was a kind of a prefab unit set up outside, with bathroom and shower for the nurses, and a little kitchen. You went through this prefab to get onto the ward itself. People from Noonan's – Bidvest Noonan, the contract cleaning service – cleaned the actual ward. There are only seven of the original cleaners still directly employed by St Vincent's.

I was cleaning various places around the hospital, and I'd finish off by cleaning the prefab before going home. Eventually, they closed down the isolation ward because – really – there were no new patients coming in. But it still had to be cleaned, because there were people passing through all the time and there had to be someone there – a doctor or nurse – because there was always the possibility that a patient would be brought in. They'd have had to shower at the start and end of their shift. So I cleaned the whole area with a D10 spray: the walls and floors, the showers, the toilets. I cleaned the kitchen. I also had to wash and dry the nurse's PPE gear.

I enjoyed the work. I enjoyed the normality of it, even though the conditions weren't normal. I liked the routine. I was seeing people. I was occupied. We were blessed that nobody on our wards caught the virus.

The Olympics had been rescheduled, but the pandemic raged on, and by the end of 2020 I was thinking that they might cancel the Games altogether. I was going from 'No, they're not going to cancel,' to 'Yeah, they are going to cancel,' back to 'No, they're not' – up and down, up and down. There was talk that the Japanese people didn't want the Games to happen. And fair enough – it's their country and it was their people who were going to get sick and possibly die. I'd have understood if they had decided to cancel the whole thing. If they'd been taking place in Ireland, would I have wanted them cancelled? Probably – possibly – maybe – I don't know. It was hard to imagine how the Japanese government could control the spread of the virus. People's lives were at risk.

The prospect of the Games being cancelled wasn't keeping me awake. We were in the middle of a global pandemic. From where I was, I wondered how they could run an entire Olympics when we couldn't even run Croke Park.

Eventually, the boxers in the High Performance Unit, the elite performers, were allowed to train in Abbotstown – in pods. I felt a bit embarrassed when that happened. I remember thinking, 'The whole of Ireland's entrapped and all of a sudden the elite can go out and train.' I don't like that word, 'elite'.

There were only a few of us at Abbotstown – myself, Emmet Brennan, George Bates, Michaela Walsh, Aoife O'Rourke, Aidan Walsh, Gytis Lisinskas, Brendan Irvine, Kirill Afanasev, Kurt Walker, all the boxers who were due to go to the Qualifiers. Zaur, Dima, John Conlan and Eoin Pluck were coaching us. We were tested every day.

There was no sparring. If we were doing pads, the coaches had to wear masks. That wasn't easy for them, because they were exerting themselves too. Pre-Covid, there could have been thirty boxers working in the gym. Now, there might have been fifteen, divided into pods. We did two sessions a day but, because of the pods, the coaches were doing four. So the coaches were stretched.

Eventually, we were able to spar. I tried to change the way I box – a little bit. I wouldn't be the best inside fighter, a Mike Tyson-style fighter – getting in, and working the body, coming up for the head. Throughout lockdown, I was able to practise that. I had the time and I felt that I was improving, just a little bit.

Dublin airport was deserted, really quiet. It was strange, but nice. We were going to the Strandja Memorial Tournament, a multi-nations in Bulgaria, in late February 2021 – nearly a year after the Olympic Qualifiers had been postponed.

In Sofia, everyone was wearing masks and all the precautions were being taken. But once the tournament started, it was like there was no such thing as Covid. I felt unsafe in the venue. There were people there who shouldn't have been, who didn't need to be there. It was as if people who would normally have been in the crowd, the audience, were now wandering around the warm-up area. I hadn't felt unsafe before, but now I felt that I was in a situation where I was going to be infected.

We knew at this stage that the Olympic Qualifiers were going to happen in June, in Paris. The draw was unchanged, so I'd be fighting Aneta Rygielska, from Poland. We'd both had a year to prepare for the fight.

What we hadn't realized was that we'd be meeting each other in Sofia three months before the Qualifiers. I'd fought and beaten Aneta in this tournament the year before.

I was a bit nervous. There's a lot to be learnt from a fight, whether you win or lose. If it was close, she'd have a lot to go off and work on, and she could come back in June, in Paris, and do the job – beat me – in the fight that actually mattered. But, thankfully, it wasn't that close. I beat her well; it was a unanimous decision.

My second fight was against a Russian girl, Nune Asatryan. She was a good boxer. She had a really good jab and right-hand shot. She was a good counter-boxer, but she moved forward as well. She was very dirty, though; she held me, and pushed my head down.

I lost the fight on a 4–1 decision, but I genuinely thought I'd won it; I'd landed more shots than she had. I was upset. I got out of the ring and I looked at the scores. Two of the judges had given me every round and the other three had messed it up, giving her rounds, giving me rounds. It looked to me like I was being done out of it, and I lost it a bit and started shouting.

'Yis should've went to fuckin' Specsavers!'

They were all looking around, going, 'What did she say?'

The tears were flying down my face. As I was walking out, I headed for the table where the tournament officials sat.

John Conlan and Zaur tried to stop me.

'Come on, Kellie – don't waste your time.'

'No – I'm fuckin' sick of this.'

There'd been murder about bad decisions made in the

past by the AIBA, the international boxing association, and there were rumours that boxing wouldn't even be included in future Olympic Games because of it. So I walked up to the top table.

'The whole eyes of the fuckin' world are watching you now and they've seen this fuckin' fiasco. Every one of us works our arses off – for this! To come out here and get unfairly fuckin' treated!'

The woman at the table was just sitting there looking at me. John gently pulled me away.

'Don't worry about it.'

It had happened two years in a row at the same tournament; I lost fights I'd actually won. The sad thing is, it seems to have got to the stage where everyone in boxing just shrugs and says, 'It's boxing – it happens.'

Any doubts I'd had about my thumb were gone. I was brand new; there wasn't a bother on me. I was well and truly ready. I was pissed off but I was saying to myself, 'D'you know what – the Olympic Qualifiers are around the corner and this Association isn't looking after the Olympic Qualifiers. I'll be treated fairly. I'll get the right decision, if I deserve it.'

After Sofia, we came back to Ireland and had a couple of days off. Then we were straight back into training camp, in the University of Ulster, with Team GB and Italy. It was a relatively small camp, due to the restrictions, but it was still a large group of people – and three very good teams. There were test matches at this camp, with referees and judges.

I fought Alessia Mesiano, and got the decision, but at one point my back was to the ropes. Mesiano was a World champion in 2016, at a weight below me. She's a very good fighter. She's technically good, but she also puts the pressure on, walks her opponent down, and cuts the ring off very well.

It was a very, very high-paced fight, punch for punch, no let-up; it was constant – no standing and thinking about my next move; I had to throw and think on the move. A couple of the referees commented on how tough the fight had looked.

I was starting to question myself.

'Am I fit – am I ready? Did it look like I was hanging together in there?'

When I had time to reflect on the fight and I'd watched it back, it didn't look as bad as I'd been thinking it had been. When I'm in the ring and under pressure, I can panic a bit: 'Fuck – I'm fucked, I'm fucked.'

When I looked back at the fight I saw that I'd gone into the ring ready to box smart, to fight my fight, but that Mesiano immediately closed the space and took my game away from me. I was fighting her fight, instead of mine. I started to think differently and to lose concentration, and stopped doing what I'd normally do – and I felt like I was dying inside. But it wasn't as bad as I'd remembered – and I *had* won. There weren't many other boxers who fought like that; she'd a real pro style about her. She knew what she was doing. So the fight was really good preparation for the Qualifiers – and that's the purpose of a pre-tournament training camp.

It was another two months to the Qualifiers. Everyone was very careful – what we were doing, where we were going, who we were with. There were the boxers who were going to the Qualifiers and there were also some sparring partners or training partners who weren't going. It was always emphasized that they were still valued members of the

Olympic team. They bought into that; they were part of the team, and they were also preparing for the following Olympics, in 2024, in Paris.

The training was very well managed. We had to stay in a hotel, to minimize contacts. Most of the time I stayed in the Carlton in Blanchardstown, a five-minute drive to Abbotstown. I'd organized cover at St Vincent's as the Qualifiers got closer. I was afraid of bringing the Covid into the hospital, even though we were very careful; and it was hard to train from Monday to Friday and then go into work on Saturday and Sunday, cleaning. I wanted to clean my own house at the weekend.

I was getting ready for my first fight, against Aneta Rygielska, and making sure that I didn't start looking past that, to the next round. It would have been easy to think, 'I've beaten her twice already – I'll beat her again.' But I never think like that.

'This girl is going to be really hungry to beat me. She's not sitting at home, scratching her bleedin' head. She owes me a beating.'

Still, there was a very specific reason to look ahead to the next round. Because if I won that fight as well, I would be certain of qualifying for the Olympics.

17

I got the jab going and kept her away with the jab,
but – my God – she put the pressure on. She ate my
punches like they were going out of fashion.

I was sparring with Brendan Irvine; this was in Abbotstown, before going to the Qualifiers. He dropped me, but I got up and we finished the round off.

Another day, I had a really hard spar. I didn't get dropped or anything, but it was one of those emotional days.

'Ah, fuck this shit – I've had enough here.'

I got all my gear off and I jumped out of the ring.

John Conlan was there.

'I'm done, John – I'm done. I'm not getting back in.'

'Get the headguard back on you,' he said, 'and get back in there.'

'No – I'm done, I'm done.'

John looked at me.

'These are the days when you learn the most, Kellie. Get back in there.'

I got back in and I sparred really, really well. Then I got back out.

'Thanks for that, John – thanks.'

Noel Burke, my coach at St Mary's, is what I call my honest coach. They're all honest, but Noel is the one I really trust to give me an honest assessment. I'd be asking, 'How do you think I did?' It's not that the rest of the coaches would lie and tell me that I did great – but Noel is that person, the one I know will tell me exactly how I did.

John Conlan is a friend *and* a coach. He's very honest with me but also very motivational. He knows what's going on in my head – more than the others – but he's still coaching me. There's a line where friendship stops and the coaching starts. John and Noel are the coaches who are also my good friends, but the three of us know exactly where the line is.

We got to Villebon, south of Paris, four days before the Qualifiers started. We always arrive a bit early, to get a sense of the place – the arena, the set-up – and to train, to check on weight.

Our hotel was enclosed – fenced in. We weren't allowed to leave the grounds. If we did, we'd be disqualified and sent home – that was an International Olympic Committee ruling. The grounds weren't extensive, but you don't need much space to get fresh air. There were seats outside, and there was a field at the perimeter fence with two goats in it. I could look at the goats, do a lap of the hotel, and have another look at the goats.

My room was on the bottom floor. Normally, there'd be two people to a room, sometimes three. It's great to have someone to chat to, especially on competition day, and I don't have to stare at the wall; we can have a bit of banter. So I was a bit worried when we were told that we'd have to have rooms of our own.

'Ah, Jesus Christ – I'm going to have to listen to my own thoughts in my own head.'

But once the competition started, I was happy enough being on my own. I'd lie on the bed and watch people doing laps – walking around, and walking around, and walking around.

The day before my first fight, on 4th June, I did a sweat session in the hotel car park. The sun was out and I was wearing a long-sleeved top, leggings, a windbreaker and a monkey hat. I did a warm-up, then I did some pads and went over what I'd be doing the next day, during the fight. Zaur, John and Dima were there, and some of the other boxers; I'd do a round with Zaur, a round with John, a round with Dima. It was nothing too rigorous. I knew my body well enough to know I was the right weight.

The weigh-ins were in a different hotel. It was a five-minute walk away but we weren't allowed to walk, in case we rambled off into a café. There was a list of who was due to weigh in, and they'd check us getting on the bus. We'd go to the hotel, weigh in, come back, and they'd check us getting off the bus, back at our hotel. After Sofia, when I'd felt uncomfortable about the lack of proper restrictions, this felt safe; it was very impressive.

There wasn't a bother on me coming up to my fight with Aneta Rygielska. I was a small bit nervous, because I'd never been in an Olympic Qualifier before.

'Get in and get it done with – whatever will be will be.'

She was warming up in the same area as me. The warm-up area wasn't very big but, apparently, they'd extended it after the first day because it had been a bit overcrowded. There were two rings, and the warm-up area was behind them. We couldn't see the rings, but there were two big screens; we could see the fights going on in both rings. There were teams from other countries there too, as I was warming up. It was great, watching the other boxers preparing for their own fights.

The fight with Rygielska went the way that I had imagined it would. I controlled it – and even when she was exerting control, I was able to match what she was doing. I won on a unanimous decision, and on my way back out I asked who I'd be fighting next.

'It's France tomorrow. Hamadouche.'

'Right – grand.'

Maïva Hamadouche had fought against the Croatian girl, Marija Malenica. I'd seen some of that fight while I was warming up before my own fight against Aneta Rygielska, but I wanted to concentrate on my own fight, so I didn't watch to the end.

The previous year, when the Qualifiers were posponed, I hadn't felt ready to face Hamadouche. Now I felt stronger. But I wasn't underestimating her. She was a pro boxer; she'd been a World champion. (Professional boxers could fight in the Olympics, but the decision whether to admit them or not was down to each country's boxing federation. Ireland didn't allow it; but France did.) I knew I'd a tough fight ahead of me.

I had to rest and recover quickly, because there was only a day between the fights and I'd have to make weight again. I just did a bit of skipping, five to ten minutes, to make sure the weight stayed down; the skipping keeps the sweat going. Then I went back to the hotel and had a recovery shake on the way; I put a jacket on, to keep the sweat going. I checked my weight when I got back. It was fine. I was able to eat. I checked the weight again. Again, it was fine. So I was able to keep picking and sipping thoughout the day. I was recovering well.

I got a sports massage from the physio, Lorcan McGee, to loosen out the body. If you don't stretch and do proper recovery after a fight, you'll feel broken up the following day. Your body's in bits – aches, pains; it doesn't matter if you didn't take much punishment during the fight. Your body is tense going into a fight; you're constantly moving in different ways, quickly. I'm a very reactive boxer; I react to what's in front of me, even without thinking about it, so I might be moving in ways that I hadn't done in sparring. I have to be very agile. The massage after the fight is vital.

I got up the next day and I felt brand new. My weight was perfect for the second weigh-in; I was bang-on for all of my weigh-ins. It was a real test of my willpower because there were cakes and croissants waiting there to be eaten. I had my Flahavan's Quick Oats – I always bring my own – with my raisins and my flax seeds. I had two slices of toast and two boiled eggs, and two croissants. So I got it all into me; it was going to keep me going for the rest of the day. I was well fuelled for the fight.

Maïva Hamadouche was smaller than me. Smaller boxers can bob and weave, roll under the punches; they can be good at getting in close very quickly. You don't have time to think and breathe and box clever, because they take the space off you. I knew that that was what Hamadouche was going to do. I was preparing myself mentally for war.

I had my lunch – pasta – three hours before the fight. Eating pasta at half-ten in the morning can often be quite difficult. I feel like a stuffed turkey afterwards; I can't move.

I made my way to the venue, and I took two bananas with me. I began to feel a little bit hungry just before the fight. That often happens. I was nervous. I knew I was going into a war. There'd be nothing unexpected about this; I knew what I was facing. It's a bit like your own execution: 'Oh, God – do I have to face this now?'

I was in the warm-up area, but there was no sign of Maïva Hamadouche.

'Where the hell is she, like?'

Then she arrives and she's warming up. I'd said hello to Aneta Rygielska before we'd boxed; we were all staying in the same hotel. This French girl, though – she had an ice-cold presence about her. She'd have walked straight through me before she'd have said hello, never mind looked my way.

'Ah, Mother of Jaysis – I'm getting into the ring with the Terminator.'

There had been a possibility that I'd get through to the Olympics even if I lost in the second round. There was a ranking system in place and I was Number 2, behind Mira Potkonen. If she won her first two fights, I'd be guaranteed a spot even if I lost in the second round. But Mira lost her first-round fight to Caroline Dubois, from Team GB. There was another back door, the possibility of a box-off with a woman from the opposite side of the draw, but I needed to concentrate on beating Hamadouche.

Hamadouche's coach took her to a screened-off space at the side of the warm-up area, and they were doing pads. It was the same thing every time; she'd come forward like a bull and throw a million punches. Did she think she was hiding some new tactic that we didn't know about? None of us were worried. We thought it was a bit mad.

The time came and we got into the ring. I got the jab going and kept her away with the jab, but – my God – she put the pressure on. She ate my punches like they were going out of fashion. She just kept coming. There was no plan in what she was doing. If I get hit, I stop and I think, 'Right – don't do that again.' And if it happens again, I go, 'Now *really* don't do that again' – because the opponent is clearly aware of what you're trying to do. But there was none of that with Hamadouche. She would take six punches to land three. Each of those punches was potentially a point, and mine were much cleaner. I was landing the better shots, and more often.

It's very hard to hear your corner when you're in a fight like that. You're just thinking, 'Fuckin' hell – this one just won't stop coming. When's the bell going to go?' But they were telling me to keep jabbing, to keep moving – because, at times, I started to stand and mix it with her. It was hard to resist, because she kept walking me down and cutting the ring off. I was tiring, and she was constantly throwing, constantly throwing – and I was constantly moving, slipping away, weaving, throwing with her, sometimes before her.

But I could hear the coaches.

'Keep moving – keep on your feet! Keep moving – keep putting the jab out!'

Because I was under so much pressure, I didn't know if I was winning or not.

'Oh my God – how is this going?'

Your corner, in a fight like this, can win or lose the fight for you. If I'd had a coach who was sounding panicky, I could have crumbled and that would have been it. But my coaches were calm; they were controlled. They knew I was ahead after the first two rounds. I was winning the fight, clear as day; I was the only one who didn't know it.

'Keep the jab going – keep moving your feet!'

I was hearing nothing negative coming from them, no 'Don't stand there, don't be doing this!' If I'd been hearing the 'don'ts', my reaction would have been, 'Oh, fuck – I'm getting bashed here, I'm in trouble – oh my God!' But I was hearing, 'Excellent – lovely – now stay on your toes!'

So I kept moving.

'Oh – beautiful!'

That fight took me to the trenches. That was what John told me when I got out of the ring.

'If anyone ever asks you if you went to the trenches – now you can tell them that you know what it's like to leave absolutely everything in the ring.'

He was right; I *had* given everything. I literally had to lean on John, going back to the changing area. I couldn't have gone another round – but she would have.

But it ended and the decision came: I'd won.

I was just delighted; I was over the moon. I'd qualified for the Olympic Games. And I was into the last four of the Championships as well, the semi-final – a bronze medal position.

I was exhausted, but I couldn't let myself be exhausted. I had to fake it. If you start to succumb to it, to believe it, then you're dead. 'How am I going to fight tomorrow?' You can't give in to it.

I went through the same thing. I skipped, again – the same routine. I knew I had one day's rest before the next fight, the semi-final. I could rest up and I'd be good to go the day after. I was exhausted but I was ecstatic too. I was going to the Olympics – 'Is this even me?' I knew that, in my sport, to get to the Olympics was to be the best of the best. But it didn't feel like me. I still felt like an imposter.

I did my skipping and my stretching, had my shake, and went back to the hotel. I showered, then just lay on the bed.

'Oh my God – I can't believe it.'

I'd been told that I'd make it, that I was good enough to qualify.

'Here I am.'

I always try to block out doubt as soon as it starts creeping in, but everyone has doubts and I had plenty. Now I was wondering if I'd be able to last that long away from home. A different kind of doubt was creeping in.

I didn't sleep well. I was tired but I was still on a high. Sleeping is always hard after a big win – and that had been a big win. Luckily, I had two nights before I had to box again.

The next day I was going through the same motions. I was

training out in the car park – to get the weight down. I wasn't too heavy or anything, but when you're in competition, if you eat you've got to train. It's a vicious circle.

We were allowed to go to the other fights, but I wasn't going. I kept track of the others online. When I'm in competition I never go to watch others fight. I go to the venue to fight, I train, I go to my room – that's it. That's my job.

But it was brilliant having people I knew there. George Bates, who was in the same club as me, was with us, and Emmet Brennan, who lived a couple of yards away from where I grew up. George was unfortunate: he missed out on qualifying by one point. Emmet's qualifying fight was like something out of *Rocky*. He was in a box-off with a Swedish boxer, Liridon Nuha, and it was so exciting. Only for I needed it myself, I'd have given my right arm for Emmet to win. I knew him, and George – I knew what they'd been through to get to where they were, all the hard work and the graft. And they knew what I'd done. We *get* one another. When George boxed, I was devastated for him. But I had no time to be too sad. I was still in the competition, so I had to stay focused on my next fight. And I was thrilled when Emmet won – but I had a fight of my own to win.

I got up at the same time, I checked my weight at the same time, trained at the same time. Breakfast, lunch, dinner – the same.

I knew I'd be fighting a Turkish girl, Esra Yildiz. I knew that she was a counter-puncher; she'd be waiting for me to throw, and she'd counter that. If I threw a jab, she might flip and catch me with a backhand, or she might throw a hook. I knew that she'd be reading the fight; she had a good boxing IQ. She was a little bit smaller than me, but she could bang. Hamadouche wasn't particularly strong but she'd made up for that with volume. Esra Yildiz, I knew, would hit hard.

I thought I'd lost the first round. I think they told me in the corner that I'd lost it. But in the second round I changed the fight. I got closer to her and started to make her throw. I took her out of her comfort zone. I wouldn't let her be the counter-puncher. I tried to make her become the aggressor. I was trying to feint, to force her to counter, so that I could counter her counter. I carried that into the last round.

It was a great fight. I remember coming out of it happy that I'd been to able to turn it. I wasn't as tired as I had been after fighting Hamadouche. I'd had the day's rest; I'd recovered well.

It was a unanimous result.

I was into the final, the next day, and I'd be going in against Caroline Dubois, from Team GB. We'd sparred before and I knew she was good. She was just twenty years old. She'd come up through the youth ranks, and she'd won the Youth Olympics. She'd already beaten Mira Potkonen, in the first round. I knew she'd be full of confidence, but I didn't pay much attention to her vibe; I just concentrated on my own. I was confident, myself. I'd sparred with her before; I knew what to expect, and I always box better than I spar. She probably underestimated me, and I probably overestimated her.

It was a good, technical fight. I didn't get drawn into any scrapping with her. I was getting in, getting out. I knew she was strong. She hit hard. But I knew what I had to do to win. Get in, get out. She fell short with a lot of her shots; she wasn't stepping in close enough to land. Sometimes I didn't even have to feint. I was able to get in fast, and back out. Her reactions were just a little bit slower than mine. Most of her experience was at underage level. Some boxers develop quicker than others, and are seen as the standout talent, because they're beating everyone around them. Moving up to senior level can be a shock, because now they're boxing against grown women. Caroline came up against my experience.

It was a split decision, but I knew I'd won. There'd been a lot of talk about me meeting Maïva Hamadouche and how I'd react, and meeting Caroline Dubois and how I'd react – because they were both great fighters. Then I'd boxed them and I'd beaten them.

I'd always been the underdog, since I'd started boxing; I'd been able to use that to make myself a better boxer. Now, I was feeling great: after four fights in five days, I was unscathed, and I was heading to the Olympics as one of the favourites. I don't pay too much attention to these things but, still, I knew it. I had to make sure that I didn't let it dominate me.

I had to stay who I was.

18

I'm on the bus, and I'm thinking now how mad it is
that I'm on my way to box in the Olympics. But I'm
trying not to think about it too much. I see vending
machines on the street as the bus passes – they're
everywhere. To distract myself, I count them.

I wasn't going to go to the opening ceremony.

'I'm here to box. I'm not here to enjoy the spectacle.'

I thought the whole thing would be distracting and drain-
ing. But then, when we were at our training camp in Miyazaki,
we got a Zoom call from Tricia Heberle, Team Ireland's Chef
de Mission. Myself, Brendan Irvine and Bernard Dunne
were in on the call. Tricia asked myself and Brendan if we'd
be flag-bearers at the opening ceremony. My first reaction
was, 'Fuckin' hell – what an honour.'

I was delighted.

It was the first time in Olympic history that each team
would have two flag-bearers, a man and a woman.

Linda O'Reilly, who works for the Olympic Federation of
Ireland, messaged me: Kellie, when you're out in the stadium, turn and give the crowd a bow.

I thought, 'That's a good idea. But it would be even better if we all do it – the whole team, Team Ireland.' I'd heard
that, in Japan, the deeper the bow, the greater the sign of
respect.

Before the opening ceremony we were all in the tunnel at

the Olympic Stadium in Tokyo, waiting to be called – waiting for ever. It was so warm, and we were sweating in full track-suits. We all just wanted to go home to the Olympic Village.

While we were waiting, I suggested it to the rest.

'Look, listen – what d'yis think if we all walk out and bow – we all turn and make a bow? I think it would be really nice and a great show of respect.'

They were all, 'Yeah, all right.'

'Great. We'll walk out, myself and Brendan will turn, then I'll give yis the billy.' The heads-up.

Then we heard it: 'Ire-land!'

It was like we'd all had nine espressos. We were straight out of the tunnel, me and Brendan holding the flag and wav-ing it. Then, a bit into the stadium, I turned a little to the right, and the rest of the team turned as well.

I went, 'One, two, three.'

And we all bowed.

We were bowing to the Japanese people but we found out later that we were bowing to the Emperor too, and that he was delighted. We were the only country that bowed – we only found that out later too. The Japanese people went crazy for it. I'd just thought, 'Let's celebrate their culture and, by us bowing to them, we're showing them that this is *our* culture. We're nice – we're friendly, we're warm.'

Walking through the stadium – it was the best feeling. Because of the restrictions, there weren't that many in the audience and it wasn't the full teams marching behind their flags. But it was really dawning on me now: I was competing in the Olympics. It was so emotional. When we got to our place and the flag was taken from us, I gave Brendan a hug that nearly broke him. We were all hugging one another; the tears were rolling down our faces.

*

The boxers had arrived in Miyazaki, on the southern island of Kyushu, three weeks before the Olympics started. We had to get used to the heat – training in it, sparring in it. You're sweating all the time, constantly losing body fluids. The sight of Japanese people walking around in jeans and suits and boots, pushing buggies – 'Ah lads, how are they doing that?' It was just so warm; it was roasting. I wondered how our athletics team would cope in the heat. At least we'd be boxing indoors.

It was the longest I'd been away from home since I was in London when I was a teenager. Before we went, I was asking, 'What happens if I get homesick over there? Can I come home, like?' I *did* think I'd be homesick, and if it hadn't been for John Conlan I'd have been struggling. He kept my mind occupied, having the craic and making light of everything.

We played a card game, Jack Change It, every night. I didn't know the game before we went to Japan; it was John who showed us how to play it. Everyone gets seven cards, and you don't show anyone else your cards. If I put a two down, the person to my left has to pick up two. But if they've a two, they can put the two on top of mine, and the next person has to pick up four. There'd be John, Brendan, Aoife O'Rourke, Damian Martin (the team physiologist) and myself. It was great craic. If you made a mistake – if the person beside me put down the wrong card – I got the chance to go, 'Ha ha – pick up two for being stupid, yeh fuckin' eejit!' There was great pleasure in that. I'd be looking at some of the others; they'd have grim expressions, trying to be sly, with one card left. The rule is, if you've only one card left, you have to tap the table and say, 'Knock knock – last card.' But if the person forgets to do that, they have to pick up two for being stupid. I'd be sitting there, hoping they'd forget, ready to pounce – 'Ha ha!'

Things like that broke the day up. We played it every day, because we couldn't go anywhere. There were even parts of the hotel we weren't allowed to enter. The USA women's football team were there too, but we never saw them because they were cordoned off; everyone was in their own bubbles.

The food was good but the portions were in tiny bowls, with about three spoonfuls of rice in each bowl. It was the same with, say, chicken – a little bowl with three bits of chicken. We were asking for a big bowl, then emptying four or five little bowls of rice and four or five bowls of chicken into the big bowl. The expressions on the faces of the Japanese people there – they thought we were bonkers.

I'd brought a month and a half's worth of porridge with me.

I wanted boiled eggs for my breakfast too, but I couldn't get them. There were scrambled eggs, but Japanese people didn't seem to have boiled eggs for their breakfast.

There was a phone call to my room one day.

'Hello?'

'Hello – Miss Harrington?'

'Yeah.'

'Are you okay?'

I was like, 'Yeah.'

'You have a problem?'

'No – what problem?'

'You need eggs?'

I was wondering if someone had told the hotel management that I'd wanted boiled eggs.

So I was like, 'Eh – yeah . . .'

'Okay.'

A while later, someone knocked on my door. It was a waiter, with two boiled eggs for me.

The next day, one of the hotel staff came up to me.

'How was your problem?'

There were loads of other people there – the faces on them.

I was like, 'What? Oh, it's fine.'

'You've no problem today?'

Sharon Madigan, our dietician, was with us. 'Just go with it,' she said.

She gave me a little piece of paper, laminated, with 'Boiled Eggs' on it – in Japanese – and a picture of two eggs. I had to hand that in at the counter every morning when I wanted eggs.

The hotel was huge. Our wing was about twenty storeys high, and we could see another one of about fifteen storeys. There was one day, we could see window-cleaners at work on the other wing; they were abseiling from window to window. I heard a shout. John Conlan and Damian Martin's room was next door, and that was where I thought the shout had come from.

I ran in.

They were at the window.

One of the window-cleaners had fallen.

John had been recording it on his phone – it was such an unusual thing to see, someone abseiling and cleaning the windows; he was fascinated by what they were doing. He didn't know that he was going to record someone falling. But he noticed that one of the men seemed to be running out of rope, and wasn't aware of it. John was going to ring reception, to warn them, but the man fell before he had the chance to do it. The man had died.

John didn't show us the video – he showed it to no one. He went across to where it had happened and told the police what he'd seen. He told them he had it on his phone, and asked them if they wanted to see it before he deleted it. But they didn't take it.

We went training after that. We didn't know what else to do.

We ordered flowers, and when they arrived I went with John, Zaur, Dima, Damian and Lorcan to the spot where the man had fallen. It was raining. Myself and John put the flowers down and said a little prayer – 'God rest your soul.' I thought of his family; it was just so sad.

In Tokyo, in the Olympic Village, I had my own room in a sort of apartment. Aoife and Michaela were sharing a bigger room, with a balcony. There was also a communal room, and a shower and toilet. The walls were plasterboard. There was no kitchen. The beds were made of cardboard. Everything was temporary. The whole thing was to be recycled after the Olympics were over.

The heat was the big thing. The mattress was made of some kind of recyclable plastic. It smelt like a wet nappy by the end of the Olympics! But I slept; it was grand.

Bernard said that we could write on the walls. He might have been joking, but I started to write song lyrics on my walls: *Black is the colour of my true love's hair, her lips are like some roses fair*. And: *Come out ye Black 'n' Tans, come out and fight me like a man*. I'd been listening to Luke Kelly singing 'Raglan Road', and Christy Moore singing 'Lisdoonvarna' – they went up on the wall too. And I drew the Five Lamps, at the bottom of Portland Row. It kept me busy, because I'd nothing else to do when I wasn't training.

When you're in competition you have to keep checking your weight. It's obsessive, it's a headwreck, but it's necessary. The coaches take a scales to every tournament. There's also a test scales that's provided by the organizers; it's exactly the same as the scales for the weigh-in. If, say, I weigh in at 60 kilos on our scales, I'll check it on the test scales and if I'm 60.1 or

60.2, that's the measurement I have to go off. We had our own scales recalibrated before we went to Tokyo, so it was the exact same as the test scales, and we didn't have to keep going off to check our weight on the test scales.

The morning of my first fight in Tokyo, I checked my weight: 60.2 kilos.

I told John when we were leaving for the weigh-in, but I knew it wouldn't be a problem.

'I'll lose the .2 just walking to the weigh-in. I'm not panicking. I'll dry off down there, check the weight, and I'll be on the button.'

At every tournament there's a test scales, and it's calibrated exactly like the official weigh-in scales. In Tokyo, the test scales were in a room right next door to the weigh-in room. Myself and John agreed on a code word that I'd use in case the test scales showed that I was overweight and needed to sweat off a few grams: 'Yeah.' There was probably no need to be secretive, but I suppose you'd never really want to talk openly about your weight in front of other coaches.

I went in to the test scales, checked my weight, and I was bang-on – exactly 60 kilos.

When I came back out, John was chatting to some of the coaches from Team GB. I handed him my bag and said, 'Yeah,' meaning I was all good. I was just happy that I didn't have to train to make the weight. I'd forgotten what 'Yeah' was supposed to mean! I went straight in to the weigh-in room.

John didn't know what I was doing. He'd been distracted when I'd come out, so he thought – when I'd said, 'Yeah' – that I was over the weight and that I'd need to train quickly, to get it down. But he was looking at me walking straight back in for the weigh-in.

I was checked over by a doctor – my hands, my face, my breathing; then I did my official weigh-in.

I came back out, and John was waiting for me.

'You're a right numpty, Kellie – I thought you were over-weight going in there.'

I was one of the last people in our team to box, so I'd been in the Olympic Village quite a while before my turn came. I was a bit anxious; I just wanted to get going. But I wasn't *too* anxious; I was quite happy, quite comfortable. I was eating well, drinking well. I hadn't been feeling home-sick. I was managing myself well, and I had John there, and Aoife, and Emmet, and all the team. I think I was the Num-ber 1 seed going into the competition but – honestly – I'm not certain, because I don't look too carefully at the seed-ings. I wasn't sure how many fights I'd have to win to get to the final. What was important was: I felt that I was in the right place at the right time. Everything was coming together. I just wanted to get the show on the road, to get into the ring and box – just get started. I don't feel like I'm in com-petition until the competition starts. But once it starts, it's as if the switch has been turned on. I'm in competion mode. I'm a different person; everything is very serious – there's no room for anything except competition and recovery and preparation.

My first opponent was Rebecca Nicoli, from Italy. I'd been doing my homework on potential fights and Noel Burke, my coach at St Mary's, had been looking at everybody in the European cycle, to help me prepare for the Olympic Quali-fiers. I hadn't fought Nicoli in the Qualifiers but Noel had been looking at her fights.

She had been at the training camp in Assisi, in February 2020. I'd done mixed rounds of sparring with her, but we didn't do a proper one-to-one spar before the camp broke up. In mixed-rounds sparring, you might have four pairs of boxers in the ring. You change opponent at every round, and there are restrictions on what you can do. The round I had with Rebecca Nicoli was lead hand only, which would have been her right hand, because she's a southpaw. I knew she was going to be tricky.

It's the morning of the Nicoli fight: my first appearance at the Olympic Games. I have my backpack with me when I go to the weigh-in, and in it I have my porridge oats, my raisins, my flax seeds, my honey (I packed a month and a half's worth), Dioralyte for rehydration, electrolytes, and bottles of water. After I come out of the weigh-in, I start to drink the electrolytes, because I've lost so much by sweating. I make my way to the food hall; it's a five-minute walk. When I get there, I grab a paper bowl – everything is recyclable – and put the porridge in, and the raisins, the flax seeds and honey. I pour boiling water into the bowl, find a table, and put the bowl down under a plate. Then I go and get my two boiled eggs, my toast and two croissants. By the time I get back to the table, the porridge is ready. I have the porridge, then go up and get a cup of tea. I have my toast and my boiled eggs. I get another cup of tea, and I eat my two croissants. Then I have the Dioralyte. That's breakfast.

I sit there for a while, chatting – to Aoife O'Rourke, John Conlan, Kurt Walker, whoever's around – about everything except boxing. I don't want to think too much about the fight coming up.

After breakfast, I head back to our apartment block, to chill out. My room is tidy; I can think better when there isn't clutter. It's nine o'clock by now, and we'll be leaving for the stadium at eleven.

I'll need to eat before we go, and I don't want to be walking back over to the food hall because that will be taking energy out of me, unnecessarily. Brendan Irvine, the team captain, brings me pasta and tomato sauce (as he will do every day that I'm in competition). I have that at about eleven, just before I leave. I'm stuffed. But I'll bring a few bananas with me.

About ten minutes before I leave, I put a bit of music on. I'm listening to songs from the Disney films – *The Lion King* and *Pinocchio* and *Pocahontas*. It relaxes me, mellows me out. John and I have one game of Jack Change It.

'That's it – we're ready to rock.'

Downstairs, we meet Zaur, Bernard, Lorcan and Dima. We walk down to the bus together. It's roasting out.

I'm glad Bernard's here. Bernard Dunne brought the women's team to life. He gave us a chance. He started sending more women away to tournaments. He brought the women's team in to train alongside the men's team. I'd talk to Bernard if I was upset about something and I always felt much better for it. There were times when I just needed to vent, and he let me. But he'd never let me overstep the mark. He'd reassure me.

'I need more sparring.'

'Kellie, you're fine.'

There was a plan, a process, and I could trust it.

'Everything's going great – trust the coaches, we know what we're doing.'

It was what I needed, reassurance – and Bernard gave it.

I'm on the bus, and I'm thinking now how mad it is that I'm on my way to box in the Olympics. But I'm trying not to think about it too much. I see vending machines on the street as the bus passes – they're everywhere. To distract myself, I count them.

People are standing on the streets, and at the corners, outside the Village. They wave. They look happy to see us.

It's a five-minute walk from the bus to the stadium

entrance. The stadium, the Kokugikan, usually has *honbasho* – sumo wrestling tournaments. It's really cool. There are huge posters of all the famous sumo wrestlers. Because of the pandemic, there's no audience; the arena is restricted to people involved in the boxing. Some other athletes sneak in, but that stops later in the week.

At first we're not let into the warm-up area, because they don't want the place to get overcrowded. We're sent down to seats beside the ring. I get quite anxious, sitting there.

'Is it time to go yet? Can we go now?'

I don't want to see the ring until I'm getting into it.

Finally we're allowed to go to the warm-up area. It's nearly one o'clock; I'm boxing at two. There's a blue corner and a red corner – blue and red sides. I'll be in red; I have to stay on the red side. I sit for a while. I look around me – I see who's there and what's going on. I soak it up.

I go to the changing room and get into my kit – my shorts and vest.

I always have my bag ready the night before – not the same bag I brought to the weigh-in. This one has my vest and shorts, my boots, my gumshield. I've brought a red and a blue kit with me. I put on the red.

I go out to the warm-up area. I take off my shoes and socks and put on a fresh pair of socks. They're thicker than the ones I'd normally wear, and my feet have more grip in them. I put my boots on, and tie them up. I've been wearing the same type of boot for nearly ten years – Nike Hyper KOs. Mandy bought me my first pair, in Sweden, at the Golden Girl Box Cup. These ones – the ones I've just put on – are red and white.

I take my gumshield from the bag and give it, in its case, to John.

I start to do my activation, to kick-start the muscles before

I start my warm-up. It's a warm-up before the warm-up. I go through it with Lorcan; it's nice to have someone else there. I start on the ground with a bit of yoga, a 'child's pose' – I push my bum back to my heels and stretch my arms out on the floor, then bring them over to one side, then change to the other side. I go onto my hands and knees and do a cat-camel stretch – back up, back down. I turn onto my back, and do glute bridges. I use resistance bands for other arm and shoulder exercises. The whole programme, unrushed, takes about twenty minutes.

I put my hairnet on. John puts the headguard on my head, to check that it will fit comfortably when I'm fighting. It's not my own headguard – the tournament organizers always supply the headguard and gloves. The headguard goes on from the back. He tightens it, adjusts it, if he needs to.

Zaur's instruction is always the same.

'Stretch your jaw.'

I don't know why he says that – I don't know what it means – but I do it!

The headguard comes off. It won't go on again until I'm in the ring.

I'm getting closer to the fight.

I start a light warm-up with Zaur.

'Jog on!'

I jog back and forth, in the space I have. I do the cross-over drill, the sideways jog, moving my arms from side to side.

When my warm-up's done, Zaur goes, 'Pads!'

It's not the same kind of pad work that I'd be doing when I train. It's tactical pads. I'm rehearsing the fight. It's short and sharp. He's not correcting me, or coaching me. That ship has sailed.

It's time.

We walk towards the ring. John has my gumshield, my headguard, water, towels, cotton buds, Vaseline – whatever he'll need in case I'm cut.

It's the same as every other fight. I don't over-think it.

'I *am* good enough, I've trained hard enough, I'm here and I'll give it everything.'

19

I'm feeling good – I'm feeling pumped. Moving
from side to side, backward and forward, jumping
a bit, shaking my arms, staying loose. Staring out
at the ring – 'I'm going in there now.'
And I hear Sinéad O'Connor.

She caught me with a shot in the second round – and I saw stars. Like dust in front of my eyes – *in* my eyes. I remember thinking, 'Fuck – does she know she's after catching me with that? Can she tell – are my legs gone?'

It lasted a couple of seconds. If Rebecca Nicoli saw that she'd hurt me, she was going to jump at me. The fight would be stopped.

'Does she know I'm hurt? Has my facial expression changed?'

I was vulnerable now. I wasn't thinking about my fight; I was thinking about what she might be thinking. I was moving – to survive. I couldn't get caught again. I had to stay out of the danger zone.

The first round had been fine. I'd known what to expect. I'd feinted, stayed on the edge, stayed close enough to her, knowing that if she moved, I had to get out of there. It was me teasing her, countering her, meeting her with the back hand – straight right, left hook, sidestep. She was coming at me with her jab, and she'd throw her big right hook. I could counter that with my left hook.

I don't think she saw that she'd hurt me. I must have been able to hide it. Luckily, it was towards the end of the second round when she caught me.

The bell went. I had a minute to recover. The minute between the rounds flies; the rounds themselves seem to take for ever.

I said nothing to the coaches. I let it go; I shook it off.

Zaur always keeps it cool. It's only a minute. If I sense that he's panicking, I'll panic. He says nothing for a couple of seconds, just lets me sit, lets me drink.

Then he speaks.

'Keep doing what you're doing. Keep your jab going – keep teasing her all the time, keep teasing her, keep feinting her.'

I was okay – on to the next round.

I went back out and won the fight.

It was a unanimous decision. I'd won every round. That shot to the head in the second round could have changed everything. But I'd won that round too.

After I got out of the ring, I asked John, 'Did you see I got caught?'

'What d'you mean?'

'I got caught with a heavy shot. Did my legs go, did they?'

'No, no – you didn't look it.'

'Are you sure, like?'

'No – you showed nothing.'

I asked a few others.

'Did it look like my legs went?'

But no one had seen anything. When you're caught with a punch like that, you've no idea what your reaction is – what you look like. It had rattled me.

But I'd won the fight – the first fight – and it felt great. I didn't know who I'd be fighting next; I hadn't looked at the draw. I just felt brilliant.

Straight out of the ring, on the way back to the changing area, I did the bit of post-fight talk with the Irish media. There were three or four journalists, about thirty metres from the ring. Then there were eleven or twelve standing behind the barriers, shouting questions at me. I don't know what I said to them, but I didn't mention that I'd been caught in the second round!

Back in the Village I had a shower, and Lorcan, the physio, gave me a massage. I texted home, and spoke for a short while with Mandy. I don't spend much time on the phone when I'm away, competing. Often, to distract me and – I suppose – to let me feel closer to home, I organize for some job to be done in the house while I'm away. This time, I was having something done in the garden. I'd drawn little sketches of what I wanted. It let me keep in touch with home and not have to talk about boxing. I had no idea what was going on in Ireland, or if there was any interest in the boxing.

There was a training venue for boxers, but we had to get a bus there. It was so hot, and we didn't want to be sitting on the bus, sweating, wasting energy. So we trained in the basement of the apartment block. There were no facilities or equipment down there. The Indian boxers were training in the basement too. I brought my speaker down with me and I'd stick on a bit of music. Zaur and Dimitri would have a little dance. Then we'd do pads – not a whole lot – twenty minutes, thirty minutes. Just light work, and going through the tactics for the next fight.

I think I was back in the Village after my first fight when I found out that I'd be fighting Imane Khelif, from Algeria, in the next round. I'd seen footage of her boxing and I'd wondered how she made 60 kilos; she was so tall and muscular.

She was a very good boxer, good on the back foot, a bit of a showboater – hits, moves, gone, but not afraid to stand and throw a couple of shots and be gone again. My first reaction as I watched her was, 'If I ever draw her, I'm fucked.'

But here I was, in the ring with her – four days after I'd fought Rebecca Nicoli.

We'd come up with a game plan. I'd stay in range and tease, tease, tease – make her throw, open herself up, then counter. It worked, but I was getting caught as well. She hit hard.

I remember her face – when she was throwing shots, when she was throwing her right hand. Later, I couldn't get her face out of my head – I can still see it. I don't often remember the other boxer's facial expression. But hers: she wanted to knock me out. She was out to get me.

She caught me with some shots, and they hurt. But some of the punches she threw weren't straight; they were slaps. She was frustrated; I was making her angry. What I was doing was working. But the look on her face – I'll never forget it.

I was delighted when it was over, although I didn't know if I'd won the fight.

I had – it was another unanimous decision. I was into the semi-finals, and I was guaranteed at least bronze. I was happy with that thought – an Olympic medal! – but I couldn't get Khelif's expression out of my head. I was a bit afraid of her. Maybe it was just a moment – *that* moment. She knew the fight was slipping away from her, and she was angry and desperate. In the Olympics, the points are recorded and shown on a screen at the end of each round, so I knew I'd won the first and second rounds. And so did she. The only way she could win was if she stopped me – knocked me out.

I've met her since, at a tournament, and she was lovely. She even gave me a hug.

*

I had a bronze medal but I was just thinking of the next fight.

'Who am I fighting next?'

'Thailand.'

That meant Sudaporn Seesondee – the woman I'd beaten in the final of the World Championships nearly three years before.

As we were walking down for the weigh-in – this was two days after my last fight – Sudaporn Seesondee and her coach were walking up, on the opposite side of the path, coming back from *her* weigh-in. I gave her the nod; she gave me the nod. Her coach gave John and Bernard the nod. Then the coach said something across at me – in his own language, Thai – and he gave a bit of a snigger. Seesondee laughed, awkwardly – I sensed she wasn't comfortable with it.

'Did you see that?'

'Never mind him – don't worry about him.'

We'd done pads for all of the possible scenarios – if she came forward, if she went back, if she countered. I knew how strong and fast she was, and what combinations she was going to throw. I was ready for anything.

I really expected her to be more aggressive than she had been in the Worlds – but if anything she seemed less aggressive. That fight had been very close, but I never felt worried this time. Right through the fight I thought it was clear: I was on top. It wasn't easy, but I wasn't being severely pressurized. I was able to concentrate on performing well, and I was getting my shots off better.

It was like a chess match – we were both waiting for the other to throw a shot; it was like we both had the same game plan. She was smiling and I was smiling. Who was going to throw first? The whole fight was like that. At one point the referee told us to box – but even then I didn't rush in to throw shots. I knew what he was telling us to do, but I wasn't doing it because, if I did, I was going to be countered. I teased a bit more, to make her throw – because she'd heard the warning too. And it happened – she threw, and I was able to counter a bit more. I was just a bit faster than her. I beat her to the punch.

The decision is always dramatic. You're standing there, waiting to find out if you've won. And this was an Olympic semi-final.

'And the winner – in a split decision . . .'

I was a bit taken aback. I thought that I'd won more convincingly than I had in 2018. Now, hearing 'split decision', I was worried.

But I'd won.

I was in an Olympic final – I couldn't believe it.

There were three days until the final. I took the first day off – and in the Tokyo summer heat, I needed it. It was the hottest environment I'd ever boxed in. I strolled around the Village, ate in the food hall, played cards, had a chat with Emmet, Kurt and Brendan.

I was looking forward to training after the day off; there was nothing else to do. In the final I was up against Beatriz Ferreira, from Brazil. She'd beaten Mira Potkonen in her semi-final. She was the current World champion – she'd won the tournament I'd had to skip because of my broken thumb. She was smaller than me, but had a longer reach. I knew that she was a really good counter-puncher: she'd lean back and come in. Her ring craft was brilliant. She knew how to cut the ring down. She wouldn't be following me – she'd be trying to corner me or get me onto the ropes. We'd two more days to prepare.

The morning of the weigh-in, it was raining heavily; it was absolutely lashing. I put spare socks in my bag, because I knew that my feet would be soaked by the time I got back up to the food hall after the weigh-in. I put the bag on, and then put on my rain jacket over the bag. I went to the weigh-in, then on to the food hall – the exact same routine I'd followed for every fight in Tokyo.

I was in my room, and Brendan brought me my pasta. I was listening to Disney music and ballads. John came up and we had a quick game of Jack Change It.

'Right – I'm ready to go.'

The rain had stopped; the sun was out. It was hot. On the way to the bus, John and Bernard chatted to me about anything other than boxing. We could see Japanese Navy ships docked nearby, and we chatted about the activity on the docks. Bernard asked me about my dogs, how they were. He has a dog too, so that kept us occupied – chatting about the dogs, showing each other pictures of them.

I felt calm.

Beatriz Ferreira was at the bus stop, with her coaches. Then Sudaporn Seesondee rocked up. She was getting the bus too, for the medal ceremony that would be held after the final. The Irish coaches were chatting with the Brazilian coaches. I kept myself to myself.

John was sitting beside me on the bus. He took a picture of the two of us.

'Today is going to be a good day,' he said. 'Today is going to be a fuckin' great day.'

'Yeah – it is, yeah – yeah.'

I was thinking, 'Fuckin' hell – I'm on my way to box in the Olympic final and my opponent is sitting on the other side of the bus. And the girl I beat a few days ago is on the bus too. Is this fuckin' great – isn't this a great sport?'

We were going to give everything in the ring, but there was no malice on the bus, no hostility.

I was counting the vending machines. I lost count after about thirty-seven – people kept talking to me.

We got to the stadium – the same routine. The warm-up area was very quiet. It was the last day of the Olympics, though I was in such a bubble that I wasn't aware of that until later. I was the last Irish competitor. I wasn't aware of that either. Billy Walsh was there, with a couple of his boxers. And I saw a few people I knew from Team GB.

The organizers had asked me what song I wanted to be played as I walked to the ring for the final.

I said to John, 'You pick a song – I'm not getting caught up in this shit.'

I remembered the last time I picked a song, in the USA. I'd let it distract me, and I'd been beaten.

But then I did pick a song. I chose Sinéad O'Connor singing 'The Foggy Dew'. John thought that they mightn't allow that one, because it was a bit political.

I was like, 'If they play it, they play it. If they don't, they can put whatever they want on.'

I forgot about it.

John wrapped my hands, and the wraps were inspected and stamped by a woman, one of the Olympic officials – to make sure that they'd been done properly. The gloves went on then, and the gloves were taped, so they couldn't be tampered with. The official checked my gumshield – she looked at it first, then she got John to put it into my mouth. I wear a clear one, made for me by my dentist. It's a good fit; it never comes loose.

I wasn't nervous. I was feeling happy – and grateful. Grateful to the people whose hard work had got me here, and grateful to myself. To my coaches – right back to the start; all the people who'd helped me. And the people who hadn't helped me – would I have been here if they hadn't made me so determined?

I'd persuaded myself that this was just another fight. I wasn't going to go in, thinking, 'I have to win, I have to win, I need to win.' But I knew exactly where I was, and what I was doing. 'This is the Olympic final – I want to perform well, I want to do myself justice.'

I was ready, waiting to walk out. I was in red, and the red corner always goes out first.

John put his hand on my shoulder and made the sign of the cross on my collarbone, and said his prayer – he always does it before I fight.

'Sacred heart of Jesus, I place all my trust in thee, all my guardian angels are your guardian angels, to protect you in this battle, to give you the strength and the courage to overcome everything – sacred heart of Jesus, I place my trust in thee.'

I'm feeling good – I'm feeling pumped. Moving from side to side, backward and forward, jumping a bit, shaking my arms, staying loose. Staring out at the ring – 'I'm going in there now.'

And I hear Sinéad O'Connor:

As down the glen one Easter morn, to a city fair rode I.

My whole body – I just feel so emotional, and so proud.

The organizers give us the signal, and I'm walking out to the ring.

There armed lines of marching men, in squadrons passed me by.

This is just great.

I can hear John behind me.

'Now's your time – this is your time. Everything you've worked for – everything over the years – look at you now – all yours. Today is going to be a fuckin' great day.'

I get into the ring.

I go to the centre. I turn. I brush my feet on the canvas, to get a feel for it. I tap my gloves in front of me, and behind me, and in front again. I walk back to my corner, bless myself, kiss my gloves.

'Mind me, Nanny.'

I'm not religious, but I believe there are people looking down on us, and I believe that my Nanny and Grandda Harrington are there, looking down, with Leo Keogh, and some other friends who've passed.

I tap Zaur's hand, and John's hand. Then I tap the padding in my corner.

This is my ritual – the same thing for years, since I was a girl, boxing in the National Stadium.

I go back to the centre of the ring and listen to the referee.

I've no idea what he says.

It starts, and the pressure is on straight away. She's coming forward. It's what I expected. Everything is as I expected. I fight my fight. The first round is close.

I go back to the corner. The other people in our team – the physio, the doctor, Jim Clover, the other coaches, Bernard – are sitting in the seats near the ring. When the scores go up at the end of each round, they're able to see them from where they're sitting. All through the tournament, they've used their fingers and thumbs to tell the coaches in my corner what the score is, after each round.

John looks across. There are hands and thumbs everywhere – he tells me this later. He can't make out what they're telling him. They're frantic, panicking, because I've lost the round. He goes down the steps, and across, to get the score himself.

I don't see any of this.

'You're three–two down,' he tells me when he gets back. In other words, three judges thought I lost the first round, and two thought I won it.

He's really calm, and so is Zaur.

'Right – it's very close.'

She's up, but not by much. I could still go out and throw it away. But my coaches are calm and this, for me, is the difference between winning and losing. I'd probably been a bit too relaxed in the first round, just trying to read the fight. I'd been a bit cautious. It's happened before – they've seen it before; I've lost the first round in plenty of fights. I'm not fazed by it. I'm not going to throw it away, let myself get caught with shots. I have to stay smart or she'll take me off the map.

I go back out, and the fight changes. I change it. There's even more pressure – she comes forward. But I start to throw a lot more shots – body shots and my hook, and straight one-twos. She's cutting the ring down. I think, 'Fuck me – she's really good at this.' She's throwing punches but I'm riding them, slipping back, and countering with my own. We're landing shots together. It's a great fight. I'm sidestepping as she tries to cut the ring down – sidestep one way, sidestep the other way.

I go back to the corner. I'm a little bit blown – breathing heavily. Zaur and John are nice and calm, nice and relaxed.

I act like I already am an Olympic champion. I train like I'm an Olympic champion. The training sessions are tough and gruelling; I am willing to do what others wouldn't do. I need a bit of selfishness – I have to be single-minded. I need to step out of my normal life, into my sport. I need to think like the predator, not the prey. I have to act like I'm a lioness. I'm the Queen of the Jungle. I can do anything that is set in front of me. I can't worry about what other people are saying or doing. My pathway is my own, and different. I'm a lioness – nobody crosses my path. If I want to go onto their path, I'll do it. And I'll treat it like I own it. This is what I am.

*

I go out and I do the exact same thing in the third round. She's coming forward, and she's throwing a lot more. She wants it as much as I do – I know that. I can't judge if she's landing more than I am – everything is rushed. There's no time for thinking. I do what I do, as well as I can.

It was over before I knew it. It was so quick.

I went back to the corner.

'Did I get it?'

The coaches thought I'd won, but they didn't know. Only the judges did.

I went back to the centre of the ring and stood beside the referee. Beatriz stood on the other side. She thought she'd won it – she pumped the air with her fist. But she did that after every round. I didn't know who'd won it.

I was glad it was over – the relief.

I remember thinking, 'D'you know what – we're both champions.'

We'd given a great display of women's boxing. It was skilful, it was beautiful. It was art.

'We both deserve to win.'

I don't think I was bracing myself for disappointment when I thought that. It was genuinely what I felt at that moment, as we waited.

I knew that Beatriz did a dance every time she won a fight. I remember thinking, 'If this one does the dance while I'm standing here, I'm going to be scundered.' Really embarrassed. What was I supposed to do while she was dancing?

I was pacing back and forth – I couldn't stay still.

I was waiting for ever – that was what it felt like. She'd won the first, I'd won the second. Who'd won the last round?

'The winner – in a unanimous decision . . .'

I don't remember if the announcement was in Japanese first, or English.

'In red . . .'

I'd won it. Fuckin' hell – the relief. I'd won it!

Beatriz came across. I raised her hand, then hugged her – lifted her.

I went across to her coaches and shook their hands.

I went to my corner, to John and Zaur. We hugged.

I went to the centre of the ring, and bowed, and turned, and bowed. I think I bowed four times – to the four sides of the stadium. It's what I always do after every fight, win or lose – to thank the judges for a fair fight.

I got down on my knees and brought my forehead to the canvas. 'Thank you, thank you, thank you, thank you, thank you' – everybody, and my lucky stars. 'I'm all right, I'm not hurt – thanks. I've made it through – I've become an Olympic champion.'

I got out of the ring.

The anti-doping chaperone was there, immediately, waiting to take me away. It was a pity. I just wanted to celebrate, to share the moment with my coaches; I wanted to ring home and to ring Noel. I'd just won an Olympic gold medal.

I was brought into a changing room that had been cordoned off, so I could get into my tracksuit for the medal ceremony. The ceremony came very soon after the fight. Beatriz was there too, with her own chaperone.

I felt awful. I felt so sorry for her. She was crying. I just felt fuckin' awful. I remember thinking, 'I don't know how I compete.' I wanted to go over and hug her. It was so awkward.

I went back out – still being followed. I walked along a corridor, to a row of seats, where the other medallists were waiting. I was sitting there. Mira Potkonen and Sudaporn Seesondee were there too – and Beatriz.

I was on my own and I was crying. It was sinking in. I was sitting beside three great boxers, and I was the winner. The tears were flooding down my face.

Mira Potkonen came over. She put her hand on my knee.

'Why are you crying? You should be so happy. Today you were very, very good.'

She sat back down. I couldn't explain to her why I was crying; it would have taken two weeks – I was just so overwhelmed.

I remember standing up, getting ready to walk out to the ceremony.

I walked back out to the ring, where the podium was – all the fights were finished by this time. The four national flags were hanging, ready to be lifted.

They called out the two bronze winners, they called out the silver. Then they called out my name.

'Kellie Anne Harrington.'

I stepped up.

I was handed a little bunch of flowers, with a little teddy bear – and my medal. I put it around my neck – I did it myself, because of the Covid precautions.

The Irish boxers were there, and some of the other Irish athletes. They were in the seats, upstairs. Bernard, Zaur, John, Dima, Lorcan, Jim – everybody. Kevin McManamon, the sports psychologist, was up there too, bawling.

The flags were lifted – *our* flag was lifted, and the Japanese military, standing to attention under it, saluted. Then the national anthem – I was overwhelmed.

'Here I am.'

20

The bus went as far as Summerhill Parade, to the
corner where the Sunset House pub used to be.
Then it turned left, onto Portland Row – my
home – and I started bawling my eyes out.
I couldn't believe it.

'I knew you were going to win today,' Zaur told me. 'Because
it rained. Like being in Ireland.'

I just wanted to go back to my room, just to sit down and
ring home – it was all I wanted to do. But I had to do all the
media stuff. I agreed to do it on one condition: that I'd get a
McDonald's. I was starving for a burger. So I got my Big Mac
and a strawberry milkshake.

The closing ceremony was on that night, and all of our
team – the boxers – were going to it. So I just thought I'd go
back to my room and pack my case, skip the ceremony, talk
to people at home, go to sleep, and I'd be ready for the hype
when I got home to Dublin. But when I got back to the
Village, all of the boxing team had stayed to congratulate
me; they hadn't gone to the closing ceremony. I was very
touched by that. An Olympic Games is a once-in-a-lifetime
experience for most competitors, and the closing ceremony
was the last taste of that – but they'd given that up, to welcome me back to the Village. I was crying, bawling my eyes
out again, when I saw them all there. Brendan Irvine, Kurt
Walker, Aidan Walsh, Emmet Brennan, Michaela Walsh,

PUFFY
Color:62-Lot:638280

EL İLE ÖRÜLÜR !
USE YOUR HANDS ONLY !

10x10
5
5

100% Mikropolyester/Micropolyester/Микрополиэстер
Polyester/Poliestere/Poliéster

~ 30°C'de makinada yıkanabilir / Machine washable at 30°C
~ Ağartıcı kullanılmaz / Do not use bleach
~ Sererek veya makinada kurutulabilir / Flat or machine dry
~ Kuru temizleme yapılabilir / Dry cleanable
~ Ütülenmez / Do not iron

@alizeyarns

OEKO-TEX®
CONFIDENCE IN TEXTILES
STANDARD 100
08.NO.47524 HOHENSTEIN HTTI
Tested for harmful substances.
www.oeko-tex.com/standard100

Aoife O'Rourke. Kevin Mac nearly missed his flight so he could be there – he was bawling, again. I thanked them all. They'd been there for me right through the week. Some of the boxers had been knocked out in the early stages, but they'd kept it together and had been very encouraging. Brendan had gone to the food hall and got my lunch for me every day I'd competed, so I wouldn't be wasting energy walking there. Everyone had played their part.

I went up to my room, eventually, and rang home. I didn't know what time it was; it was close to midnight in Tokyo. I got through to them. I spoke to Mandy, and my Ma and Da, and my three brothers – Christopher had flown home from Iceland to be there. It was great hearing them, but they were still in the moment of what I'd done; I got the sense that they didn't really need to talk to me!

'Yeah, yeah – I *am* on the phone. I *am* the one who done it – you can actually talk to me.'

They were so excited, I felt I was interrupting them. It was unbelievable.

I tried to phone Noel Burke, but I couldn't get through.

I couldn't sleep. I just couldn't sleep. It was five in the morning, and I messaged John: What's the story, John – are you awake? He got back: Is everything OK? I answered him: I can't sleep, really – I don't know what way I feel.

I'd just won the Olympics but I felt quite upset. I was reflecting, thinking about my childhood and how I'd discovered boxing – going back to when I was thirteen or fourteen, all the way up to now. I'd been boxing for seventeen years.

I went across to the food hall – it was open twenty-four hours – and I got a cup of tea, and I just sat there. I was on my own.

I sat there, feeling so empty.

239

I didn't know what I should be feeling.

I was thinking more about what other people were feeling. I'd made my family proud. I was crying – and I was so tired. I'd been awake for nearly a whole day, and in that time my whole world had been flipped upside down. I was thinking about what was going to happen next. I was so fuckin' tired.

John came down and we went for a walk, just talking – about the whole experience. We talked about the Qualifiers, about getting to Japan, about how everything had gone so well, how we'd done what we'd needed to do; we'd kept to our game plan, we hadn't been fazed by anything.

He told me that he'd been going over the fight in his head, before the actual fight. He said he'd known the outcome before it happened, because of who I'd be boxing.

'I knew you were going to be down in the first round, because I knew she was going to put the pressure on and she was just going to walk you down. But I knew, too, once you found your range, you'd be fine.'

He'd been wise enough not to tell me what he'd thought would happen before the fight, or during the fight. But he'd kept saying it to me, throughout the day: 'Today is going to be a good day. I can just see it – I know it. Today is going to be your day. I am going to be in the corner of an Olympic champion today.'

We ended up back in the food hall and had another cup of tea. It was breakfast time by then. I had a go at everything. I was eating curry at eight o'clock in the morning.

We were told to get our bags packed and be at the meeting point at one o'clock. I was thinking, 'Grand – I'll go back and have a sleep.' But I was lying there, turning, turning, turning. It was twelve o'clock and I was still awake. I was so tired.

*

Linda O'Reilly and Gavin Noble, from the Olympic Federation of Ireland, came around to check that the rooms were decent before we left. The rooms were clean, the cleanest rooms in the Village – but then they saw my walls.

'Kellie Harrington!'

All the song lyrics – they couldn't believe what they were looking at.

'Oh my God – the Paralympians have to come in here!'

I hadn't been thinking – the Paralympics were on after the Olympics, and the competitors were coming in after us.

I felt awful.

But then I thought, 'D'you know what? They might want to do the same thing, it'll keep them occupied – like me. Well – if they can read English, like.'

I was imagining someone reading, *Come out ye Black 'n' Tans*, and wondering what it meant.

There was a lot of hanging around, waiting till we were driven to the airport. On the bus, I had my speaker and I was playing a bit of music. Julianne Ryan, one of the Team Ireland physios, was sitting behind me. Aoife O'Rourke was sitting opposite me. Natalya Coyle, the pentathlete, was there. I was playing the music; we were laughing. That's as much as I remember.

I knew there was a homecoming being planned, and I remember talking to Bernard.

'Bernard, is there any chance we can move the homecoming to another day? 'Cause I'm just, like, in bits and I feel like I don't have the energy to do anything and I don't think I'm going to sleep.'

'Ah, you'll sleep on the plane.'

But I didn't.

I was sitting with Emmet and Brendan on the flights

home. Myself and Emmet tried to sleep during the first part of the journey, but Brendan kept waking us up, for the craic; he thought it was hilarious. We flew to Doha, and during the second flight, from Doha to Dublin, we kept waking Brendan up.

'Brendan!'

He'd jump.

'Are you all right?'

And he'd go, 'Ah, for fuck sake.'

Revenge was sweet.

I didn't sleep during the second flight either. My brain wouldn't switch off. All I could think about was how exhausted I was.

When we landed I took the medal from my bag, because I knew I'd need it. I took it out of the box and put it in my pocket. I didn't want to be wearing it walking out; I'd have been scarlet doing that.

I met my Ma and Da, and Mandy; they'd been allowed to come and meet us before we walked together to Arrivals. We all had a little whinge. My Da was there in the corner, holding the tears back. He'd said to Mandy, 'Jesus, Mandy, I feel like I'm meeting her for the first time, all over again.'

I wanted everyone, the whole team, to walk out together, not me walking out first. But it didn't happen; I had to go first.

We'd been told that no one had been allowed to go out to the airport, because of the restrictions. But Mel Leonard, the secretary of my club, and Ciaran Bates and his son, and Mel's wife, Sinéad, were there, and some people from the other boxers' clubs. And Anna Moore – the Mammy of Irish boxing. But when I walked out, I couldn't see anybody. I was so tired, I couldn't recognize faces I knew.

I got a lift to Clontarf, to the astro pitches beside the

DART station. The open-top bus was there, waiting. We got on the bus. Emmet and his family were with me. Emmet lived around the corner from my parents' house, and he'd been in Coláiste Íde when I'd been there. We've known each other since we were kids. We'd been in Corinthians and Glasnevin Boxing Club together. To have two people from the same place, competing in the Olympics, in the same sport – it was special.

The way I'd imagined it, I was going to be driven to Portland Row, I'd wave at a few people, and I'd go in for a cup of tea with my Ma and Da.

The bus went through Fairview, and kept right at Edge's Hardware, up towards the Luke Kelly Bridge. And when I saw the crowd, it was like I got a second wind – I was alive! There was music pumping, and everyone shouting.

'Kell-ie! Emm-et! Kell-ie! Emm-et!'

There were people running after the bus. There were people throwing flowers onto the top deck.

'Oh my God – this is just mental.'

Someone threw a teddy bear, and it hit the bus, back off the window. And someone else grabbed it when it was going under the bus.

'Oh, Jesus Christ!'

It was someone I knew, a fella my age. It wasn't a kid!

'That's all we need now – someone to get squashed under the bus during my homecoming!'

The bus went up through Ballybough, and me and Emmet were nearly decapitated when it was going under the railway bridge. We were busy looking around, our heads turned.

My brother Joel shouted, 'Watch!'

We ducked just in time.

The bus went as far as Summerhill Parade, to the corner where the Sunset House pub used to be. Then it turned left, onto Portland Row – my home – and I started bawling my eyes out.

I couldn't believe it. I was sobbing. Both sides of the road were packed.

I saw my friends Jamie Lee Brennan and Serena Brennan.

I saw my old neighbour, Mick Dunne. We'd chatted about the Oympics one day when I was visiting my Ma, before I'd gone to Tokyo.

Mick had been battling cancer. He'd followed all of my fights in Tokyo. He'd set the alarm to wake him on the morning of the final – 6 a.m. Irish time. He said to his girls, his seven daughters, 'If yis don't fuckin' wake me up for Kellie's fight, there'll be trouble – I'll wreck this gaff tomorrow.'

My old friend Sarah is one of his daughters. The whole family got up to watch the fights. On the day of the final, there was a big screen in Portland Row. But Mick wasn't well enough to go up to the screen. He was attached to an oxygen tank; if he moved, a lot of equipment had to go with him. He could barely go anywhere, the girls were telling me; he'd very little energy. Megan stayed with him, and she told me that the second I won, he stood up out of his wheelchair, picked up the oxygen, and ran out the door, down Portland Row.

'She fuckin' won!'

He ran down to my Ma's door.

One of the girls told me, 'What you done was amazing – but what we saw our Da doing was even more amazing.'

It seemed to give him a bit of life that they'd thought was gone.

The bus turned onto Portland Row at about five o'clock. Mick had been sitting outside his house since twelve. The place was getting more and more packed, and there was music going, and pizza doing the rounds; kids were getting their faces painted. The girls were worried about Mick, because of the Covid, on top of everything else.

'Da – she's not going to be here for a good while.'

'I'm waiting here – I'm not going anywhere.'

The bus got to Mick's house, and I saw him. The tears were rolling down my face.

'Mick! Mick!'

'Yeahhh – !'

I'd known Mick since I was a little girl. He was dog mad, like me. Before I went to the Olympic Qualifiers, I'd been telling him about what I'd be trying to do.

I saw my family, outside the door.

I saw Linda Mangan, Sarah Dunne, Lyndsey McNeill, Pearl Harcourt, Louise Arkins, David Grimes and my old pal Angelina – Ango. There were so many old friends, so many faces I'd known all my life – and others I'd never seen before.

Joey O'Brien, my first coach – the man who'd got me into Corinthians all those years ago – was there, although I didn't see him.

I saw Christy Dunne, from Baldoyle Boxing Club, with girls from the club.

I was so proud, to be giving the community something to be happy about. For all the little kids to see what could be achieved. It's mad, but I felt like I'd lifted the nation. I was just so proud. To have done this thing for my country, for my family and my community – and myself.

I'd thought that I'd be able to go to my Ma's house when I got off the bus. We'd have a cup of tea and chat about the Olympics. But it was too busy, too hectic. I wouldn't have been able to get near the house. I couldn't walk up the street.

So I went home – myself and Mandy went home.

Acknowledgements

Kellie:
Thanks to my parents, Yvonne and Christy; my brothers, Christopher, Aaron and Joel; Stephen Cooney, Noel Burke and Roddy.

Roddy:
Thanks to Lucy Luck, Brendan Barrington, Mary Chamberlain and Kellie.

Index

KH indicates Kellie Harrington.